THE ETHICAL BUSINESS
CHALLENGES AND CONTROVERSIES

THE ETHICAL BUSINESS

CHALLENGES AND CONTROVERSIES

Kamel Mellahi and Geoffrey Wood

First published 2003 by
PALGRAVE MACMILLIAN
Houndmills, Basingstoke, Hampshire RG21 6XS and
175 Fifth Avenue, New York, N.Y. 10010
Companies and representatives throughout the world

PALGRAVE MACMILLAN is the global academic imprint of the Palgrave
Macmillan division of St. Martin's Press, LLC and of Palgrave Macmillan Ltd.
Macmillan® is a registered trademark in the United States, United kingdom
and other countries. Palgrave is a registered trademark in the European
Union and other countries.

ISBN 0–333–94993–5

This book is printed on paper suitable for recycling and
made from fully managed and sustained forest sources.

A catalogue record for this book is available from the Library of Congress.

A catalog record for this book is available from the Library of Congress

10 9 8 7 6 5 4 3 2 1
12 11 10 09 08 07 06 05 04 03

Printed and bound in Great Britain by
J.W. Arrowsmith Ltd, Bristol

CONTENTS

INTRODUCTION

Ethics concerns attempts to distinguish 'right' from 'wrong', 'good' from 'bad' and what constitutes desirable conduct in a particular set of social circumstances. In the field of business ethics there is a startling variety of theories, approaches and philosophies, each professing to offer fundamental insights into what constitute business ethics. Over the years, the subject of business ethics expands, making it increasingly difficult to oversee the subject area. To make things worse, many of the ethics theories and perspectives propounded are conflicting in both outlook and remedies. This explains, partially, why some managers are sceptical about business ethics and the value of being ethical altogether, opting instead for a 'pragmatic' approach when dealing with ethics. The latter would entail dealing with practical ethical dilemmas as and when they arise, rather than seeking to develop a broader ethical policy. In this volume, we take the view that business ethics seeks to understand what constitutes ethical behaviour on the behalf of the firm, why should firms act ethically, and what the outcomes of ethical conduct should entail.

There is little doubt that business ethics has become an increasingly fashionable area of enquiry over the past 20 or so years. Today's firm faces considerable consumer pressure to be seen to be acting in an ethical manner, whilst legislation designed to ensure 'good' corporate behaviour – in areas ranging from marketing to the environment – has proliferated. Ironically, these pressures have been partially offset by others, including increasingly mobile investor capital, the rise of speculator-driven economic activity and rapid changes in technology and market compositions, all of which encourage managers to take a short-term 'profit' maximization point of view. Investors are increasingly able to move their capital across national boundaries, enabling them to ruthlessly shop between different firms and countries. It is thus no coincidence that the 1990s and early 2000s have seen firms placing increasing emphasis on developing 'green' consumer products, reducing waste and encouraging recycling, but also persistent financial scandals and ongoing allegations of misconduct by major multinational firms in the developing world. It is generally recognized that business ethics matters. More contentious are questions such as where the primary duty of management lies – to shareholders, all members of the organization, stakeholders, society, or the entire biosphere? Similarly, if, managers only act in an ethical fashion to stay out of trouble with the law, or to placate consumers, are they really acting in an ethical fashion at all? In other words, is a 'good' action only 'good' if prompted for the 'right' reasons. These issues represent central themes in the contemporary literature in business ethics, and indeed, in this volume.

This book is divided into two closely interrelated parts. In the first, entitled 'Theories and Issues Facing Management', we ground business ethics within the classical philosophical tradition, and go on to explore a range of contemporary ethical issues and policy options facing management, ranging from corporate governance to green issues. In the second, entitled 'Ethical Management in Practice', drawing on many of the constructs and issues discussed in the first half, we outline key ethical questions and debates facing the different functional areas of management, ranging from finance to marketing.

Chapter 1 commences with a look at what really constitutes 'ethics', the relationship between ethics and morality, and whether a particular set of ethical guidelines can be valid in different social contexts and at different times. Thereafter, we outline some of the main schools of philosophical thought on ethics: value theories, utilitarianism, rights-based theories, deontology and postmodernism. All these traditions differ greatly on what really constitutes ethical conduct, above all on whether actions can only be considered ethical if they are for the 'right' reasons (i.e. to promote the general good, rather than incidental to the pursuit of profit). However, all seek to provide practical analytical tools to distinguish the ethical with that which is not. This should be of great value in aiding managerial decision making, in matters concerning both internal organizational affairs and interactions with the broader community.

In Chapter 2, we explore recent developments in theories of corporate governance and stakeholding, and their practical relevance for the firm. The chapter examines corporate governance from different perspectives. A narrow definition of corporate governance refers to efforts to make top executive more accountable and responsive to the shareholders' rights, and to enhance value in the investment process of the company they manage. A broader, and more inclusive definition, encompasses accountability not only towards shareholders, but also towards the company's relevant stakeholders. The latter can be defined as those who have a real interest in the firm, but one that is not necessarily purely financial. In the early 2000s, firms are under increasing pressure to take account of the interests and wishes of stakeholders; the implications thereof are explored in terms of both philosophical theory and the contemporary workplace.

As is the case with 'corporate governance', 'social partnerships', the subject of Chapter 3, have become an increasingly fashionable area of interest. The term 'social partnership' is an extremely broad one. Social partnerships include national level accords between employers, unions and the state to manage wage increases, levels of social spending and employment policies, partnership deals between unions and managers in individual workplace, or an extension of traditional corporate social responsibility community outreach programmes. In turn, corporate social responsibility represents a diversion of some of the firm's resources to improve the material conditions of employees and the wider community; more ambitious manifestations would entail partnership agreements between the firm, local authorities and community-based organizations. Whatever their form, social partnerships can yield material benefits for the firm, ranging from enhanced productivity to new marketing opportunities; again, however, the question emerges whether social partnerships are worth pursuing in their own right, irrespective of the exigencies of short-term profitability.

Chapter 4 deals with environmental issues. Taking care of the environment makes increasing commercial sense, given increased consumer demand for green products, the finite nature of natural resources and visible environmental change, and increased legislative pressure. More contentious is the extent to which firms should devote resources to reducing the damage inflicted on the natural environment vis-à-vis other concerns, and what environmental concern should really entail. The latter can range from limited efforts at waste reduction and recycling, to a 'deep ecology' approach, which seeks to minimize damage to any component of the biosphere.

Globalization – including the opening of markets, the rise of global consumerism and increasingly mobile investor capital – has opened up a plethora of new opportunities for firms based in the advanced societies. However, with these opportunities comes a range of responsibilities and obligations: firms have the same duty to be ethical in both mature and emerging markets. More contentious is the level of social and environmental costs that are acceptable if development is pursued, and whether different ethical rules are appropriate in different circumstances. In Chapter 5 we explore the ethical challenges facing business in a globalizing world, and potential ways for resolving some of the most pressing ethical dilemmas facing firms operating across national boundaries.

Part II of this volume is devoted to exploring ethical questions specific to the different functional areas of management. In Chapters 6, 7, 8 and 9, we explore the ethical dilemmas facing human resource managers, financial managers, supply chain managers and marketing managers, respectively.

Chapter 6 explores ethics and human resource management (HRM), and more specifically, the nexus between human resource managers as protectors of employee welfare and as individuals charged with extracting the maximum amount of productivity from employees. The chapter assesses the dilemmas faced by dualistic employment policies between 'core' and 'peripheral' workers, questions of personal privacy, and the implications of the strategic integration of the HRM function.

Chapter 7 explores ethics and contemporary financial management practices. It looks at new financial practices, such as creative accounting, and their ethical implications. The chapter examines different schools of thought in ethics and financial management and explores certain 'ethical but legal' policies and practices.

Chapter 8 examines supply chain management and ethics. Much of the debate surrounding business ethics still accords insufficient attention to the different partners in the supply chain and their willingness and ability, or lack of them, to actively manage their business ethically. The debate on the topic of ethics and supply chain management mirrors the challenges and contradictions facing other management functions, that is, the need of management to be able to be ethical but at the same time remain competitive, and the extent to which these be reconciled. The conflictual element inherent in the relationship between firms and their suppliers needs to be recognized and dealt with. We argue that firms should not, for instance, forbid their buyers from accepting gifts and gratuities that could influence their decisions, and then reward their selling department for doing exactly the same. Further, firms should not wash their hands from any unethical actions by their suppliers and distributors. Given the changing relationship of suppliers and distributors, with more and more collaborations and information sharing, where suppliers and distributors are becoming partners in the production process, firms have to be responsible for the behaviour of their suppliers and distributors.

In Chapter 9, we explore ethics and marketing. The chapter focuses on debates surrounding the ethical duties (if any) of the marketing manager, the role of codes of ethics in marketing, and new forms of relationship between customer and client. A review of the literature reveals that trust is an important driver of long-term exchange relationships; in marketing as in any other area, ethical conduct can be extremely good for business. However, there is more to ethical marketing than simply what is in the long term an interest of business. Important questions include the nature and extent of consumer knowledge and the capacity for the consumer to make an informed decision, the role of third parties, and the extent to which marketing practice should be ethically grounded even if there seems little prospect of financial reward for good practice.

Whatever one's ideological orientation and whatever philosophical tradition one is most drawn to, it is clear that business ethics matter, for legal, marketing and productivity reasons, but, perhaps, above all, in order to provide the basis for advancing the human condition. More contentious is the question of priorities, and whether ethical questions should, at times, be sacrificed in interests of realizing other goals, such as maximizing stockholder value. However, it is increasingly recognized that ethical management has a value of its own, both in terms of making the world 'a safe place in which to do business', and in contributing to the general well-being of wider society and the natural environment.

PART 1

THEORIES AND ISSUES FACING MANAGEMENT

INTRODUCING BUSINESS ETHICS

Business ethics is, quite simply, an attempt to apply the tools and concepts developed by philosophers to distinguish 'right' from 'wrong', the desirable from the undesirable, to the corporate world. Ethics is a division of philosophy, which includes studies of the nature, the origin and the field of good and bad, right and wrong, justice and related concepts (Lamsa 1999: 346). Business ethics is the study of business from an ethical point of view.

In the past few years, there has been a great proliferation of courses at business schools dealing with business ethics. Critics have charged that such courses can easily fall into the trap of being seen as little more than a soft and easy option, lacking both theoretical depth and practical nuance (Freeman 1991: 17). Nonetheless, there is little doubt that there is a rapidly burgeoning body of critical literature and practical courses that have risen to the challenges of providing worthwhile ethical tools relevant to the rapidly changing business environment of the early 2000s. In the first half of this chapter, we explore what really constitutes ethical behaviour, and, more specifically whether there can be any clear guidelines as to what constitutes ethical behaviour that are transferable from social context to social context. This is sometimes referred to as the relativism/absolutism debate – are things like morals purely relative social constructs, the product of particular sets of attitudes, values and norms, or something that is universal? In other words, does what is considered 'good' and 'bad' vary greatly from society to society, or are there certain broader issues of 'right' and 'wrong' that have a global relevance? In the second half of this chapter we follow up such practical questions, by assessing the extent to which such dilemmas can be resolved through philosophical theory. We outline some of the main schools of philosophical thought that have been applied to understanding business ethics: the utilitarian, virtue, deontological, rights-based and postmodern approaches. In the end, it is only through recourse to the latter to questions such as what constitutes ethical conduct, and whether ethics are indeed truly universal are answerable.

As noted in the introduction, there is little doubt that contemporary firms are under considerable pressure – from consumers and governments – to act (or at least be seen to act) ethically. However, if they are simply motivated by external pressures are such actions devoid of moral worth? Proponents of the different philosophical traditions of utilitarianism, rights-based, deontological and value theories, and postmodernism will differ radically in their responses to this and other central questions.

MORAL RELATIVES AND ETHICAL ABSOLUTES

What is ethical conduct?

It may be useful to draw a distinction between ethics and moral codes; the latter are specific, and confined to particular sets of social circumstances

(Singer 1995: 2). Ethics can be seen as a more general term, denoting both ethical theories and day-to-day moral beliefs, although many make a more detailed distinction (Beauchamp and Bowie 1997: 2). Thus, moral codes differ greatly from society to society, for example, restrictions on sexual conduct or the use of particularly vulnerable categories of labour such as children. In contrast, ethics are universal; central to the human existence is some notion of 'good' and 'evil', and certain social taboos which are common to all societies.

Self-interest and good ethics often coincide, as it is often in one's interests to act morally (Singer 1995: 3). For example, all societies have some or other taboo against the arbitrary killing of healthy adults belonging to one's own social unit. However, many societies tolerate some degree of euthanasia (commonly of the very old or very young) or the slaying of 'outsiders', those who have for some reason or another placed themselves beyond the pale of society.

Law is the public's agency for translating morality into specific social guidelines and practices, and specifying punishments (Beauchamp and Bowie 1997: 4). However, it often all too easy for firms simply to refer ethical problems to their legal departments, the assumption being if it is not likely to run into trouble with the law, then an action is ethical (Beauchamp and Bowie 1997). Nonetheless, the law is not concerned with moral problems per se; the fact that an action is legally acceptable does not make it moral. An example cited by Beauchamp and Bowie (1997: 4) is the case of Pacific Lumber, the subject of a hostile take-over by Charles E. Hurwitz. Hurwitz took over the firm, in the teeth of managerial resistance, who feared that he would take a far more ruthless and short-term approach towards the firm's resources, both human and natural. Hurwitz immediately doubled the rate of tree cutting in the country's largest private redwood forest, to pay off debts incurred in the take-over, an action many critics branded as immoral, although it was perfectly legal (Beauchamp and Bowie 1997: 5).

It should also be recognized that whilst it is very easy to draw ethical boundaries in theory, it is somewhat more difficult to do so in practice. We have just seen that whilst the killing of fellow humans is generally seen as unethical, in some circumstances it is tolerated, or even condoned. Again, most societies value truthfulness; in fact some degree of truth telling is necessary for basic social cohesion. However, as Singer (1995: 2) notes, an absolute prohibition on lies may be of little value in specific circumstances. For example, in Nazi-ruled Europe, in response to Gestapo enquiries, it would be surely right to deny that you had a Jewish family hiding in your house. Similarly, in apartheid South Africa, should managers have co-operated with the authorities in the implementation of the pass laws aimed at restricting the movement (and civil liberties) of African workers? Indeed, hindering the agents of unjust authority wherever is surely ethically commendable, even if it involves regular deception.

In deciding what constitutes ethical business conduct, it is even more difficult to draw firm distinctions between 'right' and 'wrong'. Perhaps, all that can be hoped for is to make people more comfortable when faced with moral complexities (Solomon 1992: 4), and to be better equipped to deal with them. This is particularly important in that all business decisions do have some or other ethical dimension (Solomon 1992: 4).

Two of the core disciplines of the management sciences – economics and accountancy – are centred on the basic assumption that all social actors (individuals and collectives) are 'utility maximizers' (Bowie 1991: 29), in other words, seeking to maximize the material benefits accruing to themselves; always looking after their own interests (utility can best be understood as the sum of benefits an individual may derive from a particular action). However, certain contradictions are inherent in these assumptions, the most obvious being the clash of interests between principles and agents (Bowie 1991: 29), between the owners of the firm and their paid agents, be the latter senior management or the most junior hourly-paid worker. Although it is possible to argue that the clash between personal and corporate interests can be reconciled, and / or that any differences that may arise can be simply factored into the formula, in practice, this issue is often neglected (Bowie 1991: 29). However, ethical conduct in the business world will, at some stage, inevitably involve a casting aside of conventional wisdom and taking the interests of others, rather than the firm, or the person of the manager, first (Bowie 1991: 29).

Why business ethics matters?

Business ethics became an increasingly fashionable field of study in the 1990s. There is little doubt that in part, this represented a reaction to the excesses of the 1980s, to the central emphasis on individual financial gain – no matter how achieved – and the ostentatious display of wealth that characterized that decade. By the close of the 1980s, a range of factors, from repetitive financial scandals to objective evidence of global environmental damage, underscored the importance of ethical conduct in business (Vinten 2000). However, as Solomon (1992) notes, it can be extremely difficult to define what constitutes ethical conduct. An often cited example of the kind of ethical dilemmas confronting managers would be dealing with the problem of downsizing a workforce of dedicated loyal employees, owing to a cost-cutting decision by superiors (Solomon 1992).

Given that a firm is legally defined in terms to its stockholders, both executives and employees are placed in a morally ambiguous position; as paid agents entrusted with the task of dealing with competitors and maximizing profits. However, as Solomon (1992: 8) notes, competition is but one of a number of relationship firms have with each other, and with members of the wider community; focusing solely on being competitive can be disastrous for the community, and, indeed for the underlying cooperation that is necessary for any successful business activity. Indeed, the emphasis on short-term profit maximization in the closing decades of the twentieth century, characterized by corporate raids and hostile take-overs – in the name of stockholder rights – and the resultant defensive downsizing bloodbaths crippled many firms and injured hundreds of thousands of loyal employees (Solomon 1992: 8; Lamsa 1999). Instead, it can be argued that by according greater attention to ethical concerns, the firm secures its role as a vibrant and creative part of society over the medium and long terms (Vinten 2000).

Solomon (1992: 258) argues that without a sense of community and cooperation there would simply be no firm; indeed without individual and corporate virtue (virtue being 'goodness' likely to benefit society as a whole), all success would be empty and transient. However, in any less than perfect organization or society, there is no guarantee as to what virtue theorists would refer to as the 'unity of virtues' (Solomon 1992: 260): 'good' conduct is context bound, and contexts may overlap or clash with each other. Inevitably, people become embedded in their jobs or the company, and hence are incapable of looking beyond the 'bottom line'. This is often coupled with blind obedience to sometimes capricious superiors, in the hope of personal advancement. However, there has been something of a reaction to corporate excess – ranging from excessive managerial pay to treating employees as a readily disposable commodity (cf. Lamsa 1999: 345) – and many firms today are conscious of the importance of taking ethical issues seriously (Solomon 1992: 261–6).

Practice and theory

In addition, there is a danger that business ethics can be simply deployed as a whitewash, without any real changes in conduct (Freeman 1991: 12). For example, there is little doubt that claims of environmental good conduct can help sell products; however, there is often little monitoring of environmental claims, which can sometimes be ambiguous or bogus. Examples of the former could include claims that wood or paper products are from sustainable managed plantations. However, this could conceal the fact that the plantations in question may have been planted in the place of clear-cut tropical forests, or that thirsty alien species of tree may disrupt natural rainfall catchment areas, with negative consequences for human and natural communities downstream. Other claims may be simply bogus; the consumer has little way of telling for example, if tropical hardwood products are indeed from sustainable sources, or from the uncontrolled timber 'gold rushes' that are currently taking in place in countries such as Cambodia, Mozambique and Brazil. Similarly, there is a high likelihood that wildlife products – ranging from ivory to skins – may be sourced from international poaching rackets, whatever the vendor's protestations.

Beauchamp and Bowie (1997: 11) argue that there are three basic approaches to studying business ethics: descriptive (describing practices, moral codes and beliefs); prescriptive (an attempt to formulate and defend basic moral norms); and the conceptual study of ethics (e.g. analysing central ethical terms, such as right, good, justice, virtue; an attempt to distinguish what is moral and what is immoral).

Conservative critics of universalistic prescriptive approaches to business ethics argue that rule setting erodes the freedom of the individual. However, whilst it is undoubtedly correct to argue that any regulation erodes the freedom of the individual, there is little doubt that a range of practical measures to enforce ethical conduct have been of great benefit to humanity (Beauchamp and Bowie 1997: 9). For example, the banning of CFCs represents a major step towards undoing the damage to the ozone layer.

To proponents of moral relativism (in other words, those who believe morals vary so greatly from society to society that there can be no ethical universals) the bulk of moral rules are culturally specific, and an attempt to enforce universal ethical codes represents little more than a form of cultural imperialism. In other words, things are only right or wrong in a particular context (for example, infanticide or gerontocide can be justified in certain cases) (Beauchamp and Bowie 1997: 9). Asian critics of attempts to promote western democracy have suggested that it is neither in the interests of, nor desirable in, certain far eastern societies; a viewpoint most associated with the governments of China and Singapore. However, despite considerable variance in moral rules and what different communities may see as desirable, there is little doubt that the underlying principles of morality are generally similar; it is generally recognized that sometimes the self-interests of the individual have to be sacrificed for the good of society. Thus, a distinction should be drawn between relativism in judgement and relativism in underlying standards (Beauchamp and Bowie 1997: 10). In other words, people may differ on how ethical standards may be best met, but certain basic underlying norms are common to all societies (Beauchamp and Bowie 1997: 10). However, it should be recognized that moral disagreements are inevitable, and may not always be resolvable, because, inter alia, of a lack of information, definitional unclarity and selective use of evidence.

However, whether one's starting point is moral relativism, or a more universalistic one, there is little doubt that certain strictures (or social taboos) underpin ethical conduct within specific social settings. This can be in the form of law, unwritten rules, or various codes of conduct relevant across firms, industries or professions. We have seen earlier the relationship between the law and ethics; laws may facilitate ethical behaviour but they cannot ensure ethical conduct by all individuals, all the time. There is little doubt that a degree of self-policing may be desirable. For many years, a range of

professions (such as law and accounting) have upheld sets of professional standards. However, in a rapidly changing global environment, several professions
have increasingly battled to maintain professional reputations given the con-
solidation of the industry. The accounting industry is often singled out in this
regard, with the larger accounting firms simultaneously offering consultancy
and auditing services. In the 1990s, there were a string of high profile scandals
which highlighted specific cases of auditing shortcomings (Beauchamp and
Bowie 1997: 21), most recently Enron in the United States; the firm's auditors,
Arthur Anderson, also offered managerial consulting services to Enron, with
senior partners being allegedly complicit in covering up malpractices leading
to the Enron's demise. In turn, this has led critics to argue that the setting of
ethical standards is a too serious business to be left to the professions, and that
more ethical conduct can only be engendered through both an overhaul of
existing legislation and a sea-change in popular attitudes.

In the latter regard, Goodpaster argues that only if the respect for persons
is placed at the centre of our notion of corporate community, can creeping
moral disorder in society be checked (quoted in Gilbert 1991: 111). This
should be incorporated in the overall strategic vision held by senior management, leavening out the demands of corporate self-interest, profits and the
law, to be enacted out through managerial processes (Gilbert 1991: 111). It
can be argued that Goodpaster's vision is a somewhat limited one; a more
comprehensive approach to ethics should also incorporate an underlying
'respect for persons', including the organizational rank-and-file, allowing
room for a firm-wide dialogue on values and introspection by non-
executives (Gilbert 1991: 111). From this viewpoint, the modern firm is
perceived as an arena, within which interacting individuals have the opportunity to reconcile their relationships with underlying ethical values.

What does ethics do?

Singer rejects the notion of ethical relativism – rather 'do what increases
happiness and reduces suffering' (1995: 5). Ethical relativism can provide
the justification for social injustice (for example, the use of child labour,
which, moral relativists would argue, could be justified if most in a society
think it is right). Moreover, self-interested acts must be compatible
with more broadly based ethics principles if they are to be ethical (Singer
1995: 10).

The desire to promote greater equity does not have to be based on the
assumption that all individuals are equal with equal abilities, but rather on
the notion that all individuals should be given fair opportunities to realize
themselves (Singer 1995: 16–17). Some form of affirmative action can be
justified regardless of whether the beneficiaries are of superior, inferior, or
equal ability to the bulk of the populace.

In the end, ethics should be about deeds, not about sterile philosophical debates. Both Immanuel Kant and Adam Smith repeatedly emphasized that day-to-day actions should be framed by both enlightened self-interest and altruism (Freeman 1991: 19). It is from this unassailable position that these writers – and most other philosophers of ethics – postulate their theories (Freeman 1991).

DIFFERENT PHILOSOPHICAL APPROACHES TO BUSINESS ETHICS

Key perspectives

Bowie (1991: 33) argues that there are two major theories of business ethics: deontology, founded on underlying rules; and utilitarianism, which sees ethical behaviour in terms of desired outcomes. However, a further three frames of reference have had increasing influence. The first, virtue theory, is founded on the philosophies of the ancient world. The second explores ethics from the issue of basic personal rights. The third, postmodernism, would blame ethical failings on the enlightenment emphasis on rationality, and on the pursuit of 'progress' and 'advancement', regardless of the subjective human cost.

Virtue theory

Virtue theories draw on the classic Hellenistic tradition to provide some guidelines as to desirable social conduct (Beauchamp and Bowie 1997: 38). Virtue theory takes into account the nature of the agent making the decision, and her/his cultural context (Aristotle 1952: vi). Moreover, unlike, say, deontology, virtue theory seeks to get away from either rule making, or near-rules. Virtue theory can be traced back to Socrates' admonition 'know yourself', and the need to transcend traditional notions of what is right and wrong, that is approaching ethical questions from a critical standpoint (Burns 2000a: 45–6). No matter how detailed or explicit moral rules are, virtue theorist would argue, there is always a need for some or other judgement to decide how they fit a specific case (Kitson and Campbell 1996: 16).

To Aristotle, moral judgements are learned and founded on acquired virtues. Virtues are not rules, but rather personal characteristics, tendencies to behave in one way or another. There are no teachers of virtue, virtue is something that has to be infused from an entire community (Aristotle 1952: v). Initially, they are acquired through the process of socialization, but mature persons will learn to adjust their behaviour in the light of experiences of the world. As Whetstone (2001) notes:

> The excellent manager overcomes pressures to compromise even newly acquired values, at times even opposing and then changing his or her habitual behavior. Field research in the Southeast U.S. found that those managers most admired by peers and subordinates had successfully rejected values ingrained in them as youths in the period of racial segregation, adopting new habits of language and behavior toward other races.

Aristotle includes in his catalogue of virtues, inter alia, courage, temperance, liberality, a sense of self-worth, gentleness, modesty, justice and wisdom, and argued that all were required to 'live well' (Kitson and Campbell 1996: 17). As Plato and Aristotle argue, the cultivation of virtuous traits of character, founded on a suitable motivational structure, represents the primary function of morality (Beauchamp and Bowie 1997: 39). Virtue is not something that springs spontaneously from a social environment, but has to be nurtured (Aristotle 1952: vi).

On the one hand, it could be suggested that in the world of modern business – as adverse to classical Greece – this list of virtues is somewhat incomplete and requires supplementation. On the other hand, it could be argued that if managers founded their conduct on Aristotle's list of virtues, this would solve many of the ethical problems facing modern business. To virtue theorists, 'right' actions are those that a genuinely virtuous person does. All ethical actions, inside or out of the business environment, cannot hinge on absolute rules; at some stage personal characteristics must take over. The question remains as to how virtue may be achieved? To proponents of this philosophical tradition, expertise in being virtuous is something to be cultivated, with experience and reflection being necessary (Kitson and Campbell 1996: 17) – people acquire virtues by being virtuous. Having a virtuous character is neither natural nor unnatural, but is something that has to be cultivated (Beauchamp and Bowie 1997: 38); whether of course, there is room for such reflection in today's 'runaway' world could be disputed. To proponents of virtue theories, firms are only ethical if their actions are prompted by a due process of introspection as to what is really 'virtuous'. The marketing of 'green' products would not constitute a virtuous act if the firm was solely prompted by the exigencies of profit rather than an innate desire to be 'upstanding'.

Utilitarianism

Utilitarianism is founded not on moral rules, but rather on goals (Singer 1993: 3). Classic utilitarians view any action as right if it produces as much or more happiness of all affected than by any alternative action. To a utilitarian, then, lying may be commendable in some circumstances (such as agents of unjust regimes) and bad in others. Utilitarians argue that the 'goodness' of one's actions is then in terms of the consequences; ethical conduct seeks to ensure the 'greatest good for the greatest number' (Lamsa 1999; Maciver and Page 1961: 55), what is sometimes referred to as the 'happiness calculus' for balancing up pleasure versus pain, the overall good of any action versus the costs entailed (Solomon 1992: 90). As John Stuart Mill (1964: 5) argues, the 'utility or greatest happiness principle holds that actions are right...if they tend to promote happiness, wrong if they intend to produce the reverse of happiness. By happiness I mean pleasure, by unhappiness pain and the privation of pleasure'.

In other words, individuals should seek to act in such a way as to maximize the net social benefits accruing from their actions (Lamsa 1999: 346); a practice is good or right if it leads to the best possible balance of good consequences over bad ones (Beauchamp and Bowie 1997: 22). This will entail measuring possible benefits and harm as best one can, and then balancing these up (Lamsa 1999: 346). As noted earlier, utilitarianism has had a profound impact on classical theories of economics (for example, on the writings of Adam Smith), and, on account of this and its applied practical nature, has become a perspective held by many businesspeople (Lamsa 1999: 347). Prominent utilitarian theorists include David Hume (1711–76), Jeremy Bentham (1748–1832) and John Stuart Mill (1806–73). Perhaps the most influential contemporary utilitarian philosopher is eminent Harvard professor Peter Singer, who has argued that the practice of genuine utilitarianism involves considerable reflection if the good of society – and the biosphere – is to be maximized. Unlike more conservative writers who make extensive use of utilitarianism – such as Milton Friedman – Singer believes that there is very much more to social good than economic growth.

Thus, utilitarianism centres on the assumption that, when faced with a choice, the 'right' thing to do is to try to ensure the best possible outcome for the bulk of people affected as long as it does not result in a disproportionate amount of suffering by a minority; nothing is wrong which allows this, and nothing is right which fails to do so. As John Stuart Mill (1964: 6) argues, 'pleasure and freedom from pain are the only desirable ends'. However, one of the most difficult challenges facing utilitarians is what constitutes happiness. Bentham simply saw happiness as the avoidance of pain (Kitson and Campbell 1996: 7). In contrast, Mill attempted to identify different degrees of happiness. Modern neo-classical economists would see it as that which gives preference satisfaction or economic gain (Kitson and Campbell 1996: 7).

To utilitarians, then, the individual is faced with the dilemma of choosing what will benefit those affected by her or his actions the most; the maximization of good and the minimization of evil (Beauchamp and Bowie 1997: 22). Invariably, the individual is confronted with trade-offs; even a 'green' energy source such as hydroelectric power may inflict great damage on river systems. Utilitarians hold the key concept of intrinsic good, being pleasure happiness; in other words, profits per se are not intrinsically good, but, if increasing the prosperity of shareholders may contribute to increasing the overall happiness of society, then their consequences may be so (Beauchamp and Bowie 1997: 23).

Although the basic precepts of utilitarianism are relatively simple, they in fact represent the foundation of a sophisticated ethical paradigm. The latter is often ignored by 'vulgar utilitarians', seeking to defend the neo-liberal orthodoxy (in other words, a belief in the beneficial powers of unrestrained free markets). Utilitarianism is often simply seen as a costs-benefits analysis (Solomon 1992: 90). Commonly, the father of classical economics, Adam Smith, is depicted as a defender of the profit motive independent of moral considerations (cf. Maciver and Page 1961: 36–7; Evensky 2001: 497). Indeed, several prominent proponents of unrestrained free markets, influenced by the works of Milton Friedman (cf. Friedman 1997: 57), have argued that at times profoundly amoral approaches to doing business may be desirable (Evensky 2001: 497). For example, Albert Carr argues that in poker, deception and concealment are virtues, as adverse to kindness and open-heartedness, and no one thinks the worse of the poker player for this; the same should be true for the entrepreneur (Bowie 1997: 97).

Similarly, Theodore Levitt, a marketing scholar at the Harvard Business School, argues that embellishment and distortion may be desirable attributes; consumers do not only want products, but also the 'tantalizing imagery' held out through creative advertising and ambitious claims (quoted in Bowie 1997: 98). However, whilst claiming to be true to the neo-liberal traditions, such viewpoints represent little more than crude parodies of what Adam Smith really has to say. In the *Theory of Moral Sentiments* Smith stresses the importance of co-operation and trust, and the indispensability of a basic degree of social solidarity. Surprisingly, Smith mentions the concept of 'invisible hand', the forces of the market that will ultimately result in equilibrium, only once in his classic work, *The Wealth of Nations* (Solomon 1992: 86). Indeed, as Solomon (1992: 87) argues, the individual and firm should strive to be good citizens, contributing to the overall good of society, in an age when innovation was often stifled. Smith saw people as naturally social and benevolent; justice provides the main pillar of society; our self-interest being constituted within society, and 'tied to that system of virtues that makes us good citizens' (Solomon 1992: 87–9).

Indeed, Adam Smith does not reduce altruism to a kind of ethical egotism that supports utilitarian results. In other words, he would reject the view that each person is the best judge of their own interests, and that consequently people should look after their own interests, as they know them better than the interests of others, with an invisible hand co-ordinating interactions, so that a greater good will result (Maciver and Page 1961: 42–3). Smith really argues (in his own words) 'society cannot exist unless the laws of justice are tolerably observed, no social intercourse can take place among men who do not generally abstain from injury of another…Man, it has to be said has a natural love of society, and desires that the union of mankind should be preserved for its own sake, and though he himself was to derive no benefit from it' (quoted in Bowie 1991). Indeed, it is increasingly recognized that 'a society that only pursues individual self-interest is inherently unstable' (quoted in Bowie 1991). Unlike many of his later admirers, Smith remained convinced of the importance of society, and of the need to take conscious steps to promote a general social good; issues which are echoed in the works of contemporary utilitarian philosophers such as Singer.

Similarly, another early proponent of utilitarianism, J.S. Mill, stressed the importance of virtue and of the general social good (in other words the prosperity and well-being of society as a whole), arguing that a simple utilitarian happiness calculus (in other words, trying to balance up the possible social good stemming from a particular action) was insufficient to ensure ethical behaviour (Solomon 1992: 93). As we have seen, utilitarianism is often held up by neo-liberals as 'the business philosophy', the hard-headed essentially quantitative approaches that seek to balance out the material costs and benefits of any action. This has led critics of utilitarianism, such as Rawls, to charge that utilitarianism legitimates behaviour such as the rich consistently bilking the poor, as long as the rich are collectively happier than the extent of collective suffering by the less endowed (Solomon 1992: 91). However, to many utilitarians, the right of the bulk of society to a basic quality of life receives primary importance. It can be argued that the relentless pursuit of individual profit desensitizes business, and has the capacity to eclipse the most basic ethical considerations (Solomon 1992: 94).

Like most philosophical paradigms, there are considerable divisions in the utilitarian camp as how the general good of society should be advanced. One such division is between those who can be broadly referred to as 'act' utilitarians, and 'rule' utilitarians. The former hold that in all situations, one should perform acts that lead to the greatest good (Beachamp and Bowie 1997). In contrast, the latter believe that there should be certain rules governing human conduct which are not expendable, nor subject to changes by demand of individual circumstances, a possible example being rules aimed at protecting life. It could be argued that the difference between 'rule' utilitarians in particular and deontologists is simply one of style; both are committed to some basic rules governing human conduct (Solomon 1992: 253). However, deontologists are rather more inflexible when it comes to rules; which to utilatarians are only valuable if they can be demonstrated to serve a practical purpose (Solomon 1992: 253).

Critics of utilitarianism have often questioned whether happiness can be measured, and how the best action may be selected when confronted with a range of alternatives (Beauchamp and Bowie 1997: 26). Utilitarian responses have included the argument that, in the end, the choice between a range of seemingly equally valid alternatives is one that confronts all ethical theories. Alternatively, it could be suggested that this criticism is a 'pseudo-problem':

in the real world, people are capable of making rough and ready comparisons of values on a daily basis (Beauchamp and Bowie 1997: 27).

A more serious criticism could be that decisions that would be most beneficial to the bulk of members of society – for example, denial of health insurance (or even state health care) for those with HIV-AIDS – may inflict a great deal of misery on a few. Another example would be the use of poorly paid subcontracted labour, which may be beneficial to the firm as a whole, including those employed in secure contracts in core areas of the firm's business. An example of the latter would be the following example cited by Legge (1996):

> The case that caught my eye was that of a 16-year-old who was paid £30 for a 40 hour week in a garage. When he inquired about compensation for losing the top of a finger at work, he was apparently told he was a 'subcontractor'.

The classic utilitarian response – that all entailed costs must be properly weighted – does not absolve utilitarians from the task of making some very hard choices: it is perhaps hardly surprising that possibly the world's leading living utilitarian thinker, Peter Singer, has had to contend with ongoing, sometimes violent protests from religious fundamentalists, and others who find his views on the questions such as euthanasia, unacceptable. Moreover, as Singer himself concedes, utilitarianism lacks obligations strong enough to produce the outcomes that it calls for. In reality, depending on whether others act selfishly or not may shape the outcome of events (Singer 1996: 7). In other words, ethical conduct by a few may be eroded through free-riding (for example, cashing in on a competitive advantage that may be gained from reduced overheads gained by discharging untreated wastes into the environment) by others.

Rights-based approaches

The rights-based approach holds that individuals have certain basic rights that should, wherever possible, be upheld, including life, liberty and a degree of freedom to do as they choose (Beauchamp and Bowie 1997). To advocates of the rights-based approach, utilitarianism does not properly take rights and their non-violation into account (Nozick 1984: 101). What is suggested is that the need to minimize violations of rights should be built into any desirable state of affairs. In effect, what is suggested is a 'utilitarianism of rights; violations of rights (*to be minimized*) would replace total happiness as the required end state'. The rights of others determine constraints on actions (Nozick 1984). However, this freedom of choice should only be exercised when sufficient justification exists (i.e. that it is not going to infringe on the basic rights of others) (Beauchamp and Bowie 1997). This frame of reference is based on the assumption that individual rights are paramount; the principal function of the state should simply be to ensure that such rights are not infringed; the 'ultra-minimalist' state favoured by Milton Friedman and other neo-liberal proponents of unfettered free markets. To proponents of rights-based approaches, the ethical duties of the firm are, hence, somewhat minimalist: shareholders have a right to fair return on their investment, employees a right that their employment contract be correctly implemented, and so forth. The rights-based approach provided much of the philosophical underpinnings for the policies of the Thatcher (in the UK) and Reagan (in the USA) governments of the 1980s. Reflecting this, legislation protecting social collectives – such as trade unions – was pared back, although there was an increase in legislation governing the rights of individual employees. Nonetheless, a rights-based ethical approach should call for the protection of the interests of individuals against the powers of corporations: for example, the discharging of waste by agricultural enterprises may infringe upon the property rights of others downstream (Wetzstein and Centner 1992). However, how rights are defined in terms of legislation may result in a formal commitment to a rights-based approach amounting to little in practice, an example being recent 'reforms' governing groundwater contamination in the USA (Wetzstein and Centner 1992).

Deontology

An alternative approach, deontology, has its foundations in the works of Immanuel Kant (1724–1804). In *Practical Reason*, Kant argued that we should 'impose on ourselves the demand that all our actions should be rational in form' (quoted in Burns 2000b: 28). There are certain rules of morality that are binding on all rational beings; an action is only morally right if you were willing to have everyone act in a similar way in a similar situation (Lamsa 1999: 347). In other words, 'maxims should be universalized' or the social world will be reduced to chaos (Burns 2000b: 28). To Kant, people must never be treated only as a means, but also as an end (Lamsa 1999: 347; Beauchamp and Bowie 1997: 30). One should act in an ethical way because it is one's duty, regardless of the consequences (Kitson and Campbell 1996: 13). Kantianism lays down obligations strong enough not be self-defeating, solving the problem of destructive individual 'free riding' (a problem that, as we have seen, plagues utilitarianism) in the face of co-operative action (Kitson and Campbell 1996: 15).

Of course, moral problems in the real world are extremely complex. Above all, there is the problem of uncertainty, and what really constitutes right and wrong (Lamsa 1999: 347). A decision to downsize may for example be a product of forces beyond the manager's control, and may be best for those staff members who are retained, yet may also inflict great misery on those made redundant (Lamsa 1999: 347). As Kant (2000: 55) argues, human nature is ultimately fallible and it is impossible to ensure perfect outcomes 'from the warped wood of human nature' (Kant 2000: 55). A way out of such moral dilemmas is often to behave according to custom, which provides useful moral benchmarks (Lamsa 1999: 347).

To Kant, motives for actions are critical. People should make the right decisions for the right reasons; if people are honest only because honesty pays, honesty itself is cheapened (Beauchamp and Bowie 1997: 30). In other words, if a firm acts in an ethical fashion to help it market its goods and services, and hence enhance profits, such actions are devoid of moral worth. Absolute morality is a categorical imperative with social interaction and civil society being dependent on moral action by all (Kant, quoted in Burns 2000b: 28). In other words, managers are not really acting ethically at all, if they are simply prompted to do so out of fear of prosecution or by consumer pressures. This is not a distinction that would necessarily trouble those in the utilitarian camp; to the latter, any increase in overall happiness, regardless of the rationale underlying the actions that led to this, would be desirable.

Kant believed that actions should respect underlying moral law; a person's motives should reflect a recognition of a duty to act – morality provides a rational framework of rules, which constrains and guides people (Beauchamp and Bowie 1997: 33; Kant 2000: 54–5). Whilst certainly detailed, Kant's writings are somewhat open ended and incomplete; contemporary deontologists use Kant's notion of respect for persons as a ground for providing ethical theories of justice and rights, and for distinguishing the desirable from the undesirable (Beauchamp and Bowie 1997: 33).

Ultimately, deontology hinges on a system of rules. This has led critics to argue that deontology is overly inflexible, any moral ambiguities may only be resolved by finding ever more complicated or specific rules, and by ranking them in a hierarchical way, so that they do not conflict with each other (Singer 1993: 3). However, empirical research would seem to indicate that many managers do approach ethical decision making from what is effectively a deontological starting point, an example being Menguc's (1998) survey of Turkish firms.

Postmodern ethics

Critics of postmodernism have argued that this school of thought is fundamentally ethical, representing a fractured localist rejection of universal standards governing behaviour (Lash and Friedman 1992: 8). However, postmodernism shares with conservative philosophers such as Michael Oakeshott (1983) a fundamental distaste for universalistic notions of rationality that have led to the prioritization of 'development and progress' irrespective of the human costs involved. Moreover, the desire of individual agents to maximize the benefits accruing to themselves – the foundation of the modernist project – serves to erode the very moral standards that would make modernity viable and sustainable (Friedman 1992: 356).

To Zygmaunt Baumann (1993), the unprecedented human rights abuses of the twentieth century, coupled with wide-scale environmental degradation, reflect the limitations of modernist ethical theories, be they utilitarian or deontological; rigid notions of reason or general good have been imposed, notions that take little accounts of diversity and the real needs of the mass of society at local level. Postmodernists would argue that the modern work organization represents little more than an 'apparatus of capture', a stultifying environment 'overcoding' rationalist norms, repressing individual creativity and expressiveness (Deleuze and Guattari 1988: 380).

In contrast to the assumption of ultimate social progress that underlies much of the modernist project, postmodernism makes no claims as to the inevitability of a better life. Deleuze and Guattari (1988: 380) assert that it is possible to cast aside the universalistic rationalist codes governing conduct; individuals or micro-collectives can, and will, continue to seek to escape the homogenizing power of the status quo, constructing particularistic ethical realities more appropriate to their needs. Postmodernists have little to offer managers seeking guidelines or tools for dealing with ethical dilemmas. Rather, they argue that contemporary society – and individual work organizations – are inherently repressive environments; nonetheless, the potential for liberatory action at grassroots level persists.

SUMMARY

The field of business ethics applies the tools of philosophy to understand the day-to-day ethical challenges facing modern work organizations. After highlighting a number of general ethical quandaries, we have explored and highlighted several distinct philosophical traditions that provide insights of relevance to the modern firm. These range from postmodernism – which seeks to provide a critique of contemporary social life rather than explicit ethical guidelines – in sharp contrast to the rather more pragmatic costs-benefits approach of the utilitarians. Nonetheless, each of the approaches highlighted has some merit in providing practical analytical tools for understanding the nature of contemporary ethical dilemmas, be they in terms of core internal managerial functions or relations with the broader community, or, indeed, the natural environment.

ISSUES

....

This chapter seeks to define business ethics, and locates it within the philosophical tradition. Key questions include:

- How can business ethics best be defined?
- Can one ever talk of absolute ethical standards? Why?
- What is deontology? How do deontologists define ethical conduct?
- What is the rights-based perspective? How do followers of this school of thought define ethical conduct?
- What is the utilitarian perspective? How do followers of this school of thought define ethical conduct?
- What is the postmodern view of ethics? How do followers of this school of thought define ethical conduct?

FURTHER READING

Beauchamp, T. and Bowie, N. 1997. 'Ethical theory and business practice', Beauchamp, T. and Bowie, N. (eds), *Ethical Theory and Business*. Upper Saddle River, NJ: Prentice Hall. This article provides a useful linkage between theories of ethics and the realities of the corporate world. The other contributions in this edited volume provide a range of interesting perspectives on business ethics.

Burns, R. and Raymond-Pickard, H. (eds). 2000. *Philosophies of History*. Oxford: Blackwell. An excellent general introduction to main streams in the western philosophical tradition. Includes original excerpts from the writings of key philosophers.

Singer, P. 1995. *Practical Ethics*. Cambridge: Cambridge University Press. An original and highly readable perspective on the problems of applying ethical constructs to the real world. Although Singer is writing from a utilitarian perspective, he also discusses alternative philosophical traditions.

CORPORATE GOVERNANCE

In this chapter our purpose is to show the relevance of corporate governance and stakeholder concepts to business ethics. While Friedman (1992) argues that the only 'ethical' role of the firm is to take care of its shareholders, more recent thinking provides insights into the inappropriateness of this viewpoint. The roots of both corporate governance and the concept of 'stakeholder' are central issues in contemporary debates on business ethics. 'Stakeholder' commonly includes all that are affected by, or can affect, the firm's activities, including not just managers, shareholders and employees, but also representatives of the broader community as well. Understanding these concepts and the current debates around them should enhance our understanding of the ethical challenges facing businesses nowadays. The chapter is divided into two parts. Part one looks at corporate governance, part two examines different stakeholder theories and their relevance to business ethics.

CORPORATE GOVERNANCE AND BUSINESS ETHICS

'Evolving regulatory requirements, increased media attention and mounting public scrutiny have pried open boardroom doors to challenge directors with expanding responsibilities and concerns that go far beyond the bottom line... in these bygone days "corporate governance" was an arcane, somewhat esoteric term known only to boardroom lawyers and business school academics. But now, corporate governance is a topic that dances through the business pages and sometimes stomps gracelessly over the pages of newspapers with threats of lawsuits against directors and officers, public concern over corporate ethics...' (Brown 1994).

What is corporate governance?

Just what constitutes corporate governance is still a topic of debate. The term 'corporate governance' was rarely encountered before the 1990s (Keasey *et al.* 1997). Its rapid and wide adoption resulted in inconsistent usage of the term. In its narrowest sense, corporate governance can be viewed as a system, made up of a set of arrangements, by which business corporations are directed and controlled. A narrow definition of corporate governance refers to efforts to make top executive more accountable and responsive to the shareholders' rights, and enhance value in the investment process of the company they manage. A broader, and more inclusive definition, encompasses accountability towards not only shareholders, but also the company's relevant stakeholders. According to the OECD (1999):

> The corporate governance structure specifies the distribution of rights and responsibilities among different participants in the corporation, such as, the board, managers, shareholders and other stakeholders, and spells out the rules and procedures for making decisions on corporate affairs.

At the centre of a firm's governance is the board of directors. Its overriding responsibilities are to balance diverging interests and ensure the long-term viability of the firm. A firm may make formal provision for a stakeholder voice at board level; an example would be the widespread practice of having employee directors in Germany (for example, on the board of Volkswagen).

Why corporate governance now?

At least three factors are behind the recent increase in the importance of corporate governance in academic and professional business circles.

1. *Separations between ownership and control.* In the past most companies were managed by their owners or closely monitored by a small number of shareholders. Today, however, most people in Western countries own shares. Koehn (2001) reported that studies in the United States have shown that the business section of newspapers is now the first page read by more than 25 per cent of readers. As a result, the way companies govern themselves has come to the forefront of public scrutiny, because the latter has a stake in the way companies are managed.
2. *The birth of the supernational corporations.* Recent changes in the global business environment such as the end of the Cold War, global economic liberalism, the economic conglomeration of Western Europe, the rapid advancement in technology, and the explosion of e-commerce shifted the power towards large global corporations. Chang and Ha (2001) note that 'as the supernational corporation becomes an increasingly large factor in the world, a question arises as to how far it has a responsibility to maintain the framework of the society in which it operates and how far it should reflect society's priorities in addition to its own commercial priorities'. Many transnational corporations (TNCs) are richer and more powerful than some states and regions. For instance, Chang and Ha (2001: 33) note that the total revenue of Mitsubishi, a giant corporate *keiretsu* of Japan, exceeds the gross domestic product (GDP) of South Korea, whilst the Citi Group's revenue exceeds the total output of India. Microsoft is bigger than the Netherlands, GM is bigger than Turkey, Philip Morris is larger than New Zealand, and Wal-Mart is bigger than Israel. The combined revenues of GM and Ford exceed the combined GDP for all of sub-Saharan Africa. In fact, 51 of the 100 largest economies in the world are corporations. Top 500 corporations account for nearly 30 per cent of the world's total economic output and 70 per cent of the world-wide trade (Chang and Ha 2001). Notwithstanding their power and influence, these corporations, and more precisely their managers, are not chosen by the people who work for them or the communities that are affected by them. If these companies are managed badly or act irresponsibly, the results go beyond the fences of these companies and affect shareholders, employees, suppliers and whole communities and sometimes the political stabil-

ity of the country. In simple terms, we cannot leave the management of these global corporations solely to the consciences of their managers and the influence of their shareholders.

3. *Increase in reported corporate failure and crisis.* There has been an increase recently in reported failure and crisis of well-known companies such as the Maxwell Group and its implications on the pension fund of the Mirror Group newspapers, the collapses of the Barings Bank and the Bank of Credit and Commerce International. All the latter examples were a result of management incompetence, fraud and abuse of power. In addition, a large body of research on organizational failure provides evidence to suggest that top management attitudes and behaviour are often the cause of such failure (Cameron *et al.* 1988b). This would include a reluctance to abandon failed strategies and routines (Staw 1981; Bateman and Zeithaml 1988), a lack of objectivity as to their personal weaknesses and strengths (Zajac and Bazerman 1991), management malfunctioning (Argenti 1976), strategic paralysis (D'Aveni 1989, 1990), 'rigidity effects' (Staw *et al.* 1981) and chronic structural inertia (Hannan and Freeman 1984). Literature indicates that even successful companies are susceptible to crisis for a plethora of reasons. Miller (1990) noted that 'success can breed over confidence and arrogance' by management. Ranft and O'Neill (2001: 126) argued that with business success, high-flying firms, in the face of competitive pressures, develop a form of 'cautious conservatism and perhaps arrogant disdain'. This is explained by observing that management often formulates heuristic programmes for dealing with recurring problems, and these programmes remain in use even after the situations they fit have faded away (Starbuck and Hedberg 1977: 250). This often results in organizational inertia (Kelly and Amburgey 1991; Behn 1977; Cyert 1978). Kelly and Amburgey (1991) note that:

> Overtime successful routines develops into habits. As habits, the routines become traditions, and hence, the effect of preserving the firms way of doing things. As a result organizations that were the most successful in the past become the most vulnerable to failure in the future, because they are conditioned to exploit their advantages, and less likely to explore new ones.

Larson and Clute (1979) conclude that the characteristics shared by failed firms are directly related to personal decision-based characteristics of managers. Similarly, Argenti (1976) has identified as causes for failure, impulsive decisions that extended the organization's assets, a failure to respond to change, executives who are either too powerful or poorly informed, and the taking of unnecessary risks. Starbuck *et al.* (1978) identified a source of a crisis in the misperceptions of organizational top management members. Barmash (1973: 299) notes that:

Corporations are managed by men; and men, never forget, manage organizations to suit themselves. Thus corporate calamities are calamities created by men.

Macoby (2000) describes how visionary managers can frequently be narcissistic in their behaviour and increase the risk of failure when business conditions change. When faced with a crisis, these narcissist leaders isolate themselves from the advice of others, ignore words of caution, interpret criticisms as threat, and frequently become myopic in their views (Macoby 2000). This behaviour and attitudes foster hubris because of exaggerated pride, self-confidence, or arrogance.

According to Keasey *et al.* (1997):

Corporate governance has become a focus of attention because of the widely articulated concerns that the contemporary monitoring and control of publicly held corporations in the UK and USA is seriously defective.

They argue that these concerns which are often coupled with 'unfavourable comparisons' of the Anglo-American socio-economic development with that achieved in Japan and rest of Western Europe, and specifically the conclusion that the Japanese and German governance structures 'would deliver superior national performance' led to the re-examination of the corporate governance in the UK and the United States.

Corporate governance and the balancing of divergent interests

As it will be seen later in the discussion of stakeholders, often the interests of those who have control over a firm, i.e. those of management, may differ from the interests of those who supply the firm with external finance, legitimacy and other critical resources. Felo (2001) notes that 'corporate governance structures can sometimes lead to conflict between the interest of directors and shareholders'. Take for instance, the diverging interests of those in control with those who supply the firm with external finance. The latter may own the company, whilst the former manage it. Put simply, there is a separation between ownership and control, and 'insiders' and 'outsiders'. As discussed earlier, those in control are often perceived to be responsible for failure, and sometimes abuse their power. The media is full of stories of managers who misuse their position to misappropriate economic and social benefits, often at the expense of the long-term performance or even the survival of the company. As a result outsiders want a mechanism by which they could protect their interests from opportunistic behaviour or incompetence of managers or controlling shareholders.

A FRAMEWORK FOR CORPORATE GOVERNANCE

There is no one best governance model. The governance depends on the ownership structure, corporate sector and, when dealing internationally, national corporate governance systems and cultural values and norms. For instance, for a publicly traded company with widely dispersed shareholding, the challenge is for outsider stakeholders to control the performance of managers. In this case, managers have strong control because shareholders are widely dispersed and therefore it is hard, if not impossible, for the latter to control or influence the former's activities. In this case, outsiders can influence governance indirectly by setting rules for selecting directors and provide them with enough power to ensure that they will monitor managers' activities, behaviours and performance effectively. By contrast, for a closely held company with a controlling shareholder and a minority of outside shareholders, the manager is constantly under the control and scrutiny of the controlling shareholder. The challenge here is preventing the controlling shareholder from extracting self-benefits from the company and controlling it as their personal property by disregarding minority shareholders' rights. In the latter instance, the company should develop governance mechanisms to protect minority shareholders' rights and limit the controlling shareholder's power.

Although globalization is bringing harmonization to the global corporate governance systems, there is still a strong divergence between the systems. For instance, the UK and US corporate governance models focus on dispersed controls, whereas, the Japanese and German models reflect a more concentrated ownership structure (we will return to this point later). The OECD conducted a number of reviews of corporate governance regimes in specific countries. As a result, the OECD (1999) proposed principles of corporate governance (listed below). Nevertheless, the OECD states clearly that these principles are 'non-binding and do not aim at detailed prescriptions for national legislation. They can be used by policy makers, as they examine and develop their legal and regulatory frameworks for corporate governance that reflect their own economic, social, legal and cultural circumstances and by market participants as they develop their own practices' (OECD, 1999). The principles, the OECD suggests, can be a useful point of reference both for member countries as well as many emerging markets and economies in transition. The report noted that not only do the principles provide a benchmark for internationally accepted standards, they also offer a solid platform for analysis and practices in individual countries taking into account country-specific circumstances, such as legal and cultural traditions. Below is a summary of the OECD principles:

- *The rights of shareholders*. The corporate governance framework should protect shareholders' rights. These rights include the right to participate in the management of the company disproportionate to their equity ownership, have relevant information about the company's state of affairs, be involved in decisions concerning fundamental corporate changes, have the opportunity to participate effectively and vote in general shareholder meetings and should be informed of the rules, including voting procedures, that govern general shareholder meetings.

- *The equitable treatment of shareholders.* The corporate governance framework should ensure the equitable treatment of all shareholders, including minority and foreign shareholders. All shareholders should have the opportunity to obtain effective redress for violation of their rights. Specifically, all shareholders of the same class should be treated equally, and insider trading and abusive self-dealing should be prohibited.
- *The role of stakeholders in corporate governance.* The corporate governance framework should recognize the rights of stakeholders as established by law and encourage active cooperation between corporations and stakeholders in creating wealth, jobs and the sustainability of financially sound enterprises. The corporate governance framework should assure that the rights of stakeholders that are protected by law are respected; stakeholders should have the opportunity to obtain effective redress for violation of their rights; the corporate governance framework should permit performance-enhancing mechanisms for stakeholder participation.
- *Disclosure and transparency.* The corporate governance framework should ensure that timely and accurate disclosure is made on all material matters regarding the corporation, including the financial situation, performance, ownership and governance of the company.
- *The responsibilities of the board.* The corporate governance framework should ensure the strategic guidance of the company, the effective monitoring of management by the board, and the board's accountability to the company and the shareholders. Board members should act on a fully informed basis, in good faith, with due diligence and care, and in the best interest of the company and the shareholders. And where board decisions may affect different shareholder groups differently, the board should treat all shareholders fairly.
- *The board should be able to exercise objective judgement on corporate affairs independently, in particular, from management.* Boards should consider assigning a sufficient number of non-executive board members capable of exercising independent judgement to tasks where there is a potential for conflict of interest. Examples of such key responsibilities are financial reporting, nomination and executive and board remuneration.

In the UK, the publication of the Cadbury Report in 1992 drew attention to the concern with the 'proper' governance of organizations; and in particular the governance of public, quoted companies. The stated objective of the Committee was:

To help to raise the standards of corporate governance and the level of confidence in financial reporting and auditing by setting out clearly what it sees as the respective responsibilities of those involved and what it believes is expected of them.

The Committee concluded that the recommendations in the final report 'will involve a sharper sense of accountability and responsibility all round' (Report of the Committee on the Financial Aspects of Corporate Governance 1992). The report argued for clearly accepted division of responsibilities at the head of a company, which will ensure a balance of power and authority, such that no individual has unfettered powers of decision. This reflects UK practice historically where the chief executive's and chairman's position are held by two people. The chairman chairs the board and oversees external communications with large investors and government, presenting the corporation's public face. The CEO attends to executive and operational aspects – coordinating the work of other executive directors and running the company internally. This separation is a common UK model whereas the North American model tends to position one person in a combined role. In Japan, where the concept of the company as a community dominates, the system puts trust in management who traditionally seek profit for pluralist oriented stakeholders rather that the traditional Western approach of maximizing profit for shareholders. Generally, the Japanese corporate governance system consists of a dual structure: the board of directors, which carries out the functions of strategic decision making; and the board of editors, which audits management's execution of business activities. It is worth mentioning that the latter body does only *ex post facto* auditing, and tends to distance itself from the strategic and day-to-day management process. Even the board of directors does not have the power to take strategic decisions which are reserved for the management board which includes board and directors as well as independent, non-executive directors who have no direct (financial) interests in the company and who should comprise a majority on the board.

CORPORATE GOVERNANCE AND STAKEHOLDER THEORY

While literature on corporate governance has focused primarily on the rights of shareholders, stakeholder theory takes a broader view. Stakeholder theory contrasts the traditional view which asserts that the primary function of the firm is to maximize the return on investments to the owners of the business, that is, the shareholders (Friedman 1970). According to the stakeholder theory, the firm needs to consider the interests of 'all' groups affected by the firm. Stakeholder theory is an important and commonly used framework for business ethics (Gibson 2000; Caroll 1993; Weiss 1994). Freeman (1984) asserts that stakeholder theory is a promising framework for business ethics because it acknowledges a 'plurality of values'.

Since Freeman's (1984) landmark book, *Strategic Management: A Stakeholder Approach*, the topic has been the subject of a lively debate in the literature, several special journal issues and books have been published on the topic and numerous conferences and academic seminars have taken place. Much of the debate centres on the definition of stakeholders, and whether or not management's ability to satisfy one group of stakeholders comes at the expense of their ability to satisfy another (Strong *et al.* 2001), and how to reconcile competing stakeholders.

Defining a broad concept such as stakeholder is somewhat problematic. Over the years several definitions have been proposed, most encompassing the general definition provided earlier in this chapter. Literature divides stakeholders into primary and secondary stakeholders. Primary stakeholders are those who have a formal, often official, or contractual relationship with the firm such as suppliers, employees, shareholders, managers and so forth. All others are classified as secondary stakeholders having a loose contract with the firm (Carroll 1993). A widely quoted classic definition of stakeholders is that proposed by Freeman (1984: 46):

A stakeholder in an organization is any group or individual who can affect or is affected by the achievement of the organization's objectives.

Several authors have contested Freeman's definition; it has been criticized for being too broad (does it include trees and animals for example?) or too narrow (it does not include invisible stakeholder who are indirectly affected by the firm). Nonetheless, most researchers have used a variation of Freeman's definition of a stakeholder (cf. Clarkson 1995; Frooman 1999). According to Clarkson (1995) 'primary stakeholder groups typically are comprised of stakeholders and investors, employees, customers, together with what is defined as the public stakeholder group: the government and communities that provide infrastructures and markets, whose laws and regulations must be obeyed, and to whom taxes and other obligations may be due'. To this list, Donaldson and Preston (1995) add trade associations and environmental groups.

As will be seen later, the power and influence of secondary stakeholders dictate the type of relationship the firm wishes to establish with them. Donaldson and Preston (1995) stress the distinction between influencers and stakeholders. They noted that 'some actors in the enterprise (e.g. large investors) may be both, but some recognizable stakeholders (e.g. the job applicants) have no influence, and some influencers (e.g. the media) have no stake'.

The absence of any real consensus on the definition of stakeholders in the burgeoning literature on the subject is symptomatic of the whole debate on the stakeholder concept. Freeman and Gilbert (1988) argue that the stakeholder theory or concept is strongly linked to business ethics and specifically to moral principles. Stakeholder theory proposes that firms go beyond the traditional narrow focus on shareholders' interests and often short-term profits, and consider the wider impact of their activities on all affected parties, i.e. their stakeholders. According to the stakeholder theory, firms, in the long term benefit more from a non-adversarial relationship with stakeholders rather than focusing on short-term shareholder interest. Clarkson (1995) argues that a firm's survival and continuing success depends upon the ability of its management to create sufficient wealth, values or satisfaction for all primary stakeholder groups.

The foundation of the concept of stakeholder are the relationships and interactions within the firm, and between it and others (Lampe, 2001). These interactions may produce a win–loss outcome, in that improved managerial performance in one stakeholder group could come at the expense of the performance of another group. De Castro *et al.* (1996), for instance, found that wealth creation strategies in the privatization of state-owned enterprises resulted in losses for the employee stakeholders and gains to the ownership group (quoted in Strong *et al.* 2001). In similar vein, Laban and Wolf (1993) argue that outside investors are less likely to provide capital to firms that have powerful employees. Similarly, McDonald (1993) notes that when employee groups become powerful, labour peace is valued above all else, leading to decline in customer service and a disregard for profitability. Jawahar and McLaughlin (2001) argue that:

> Organizations are unlikely to fulfil all their responsibilities they have toward each primary stakeholder group. Instead, they are likely to fulfil economic and all non-economic responsibilities of some primary stakeholders but not others and, over time, to fulfil responsibilities relative to each stakeholder to varying extents.

The above literature seems to indicate that conflict between an organization and its stakeholders is inevitable. Several scholars argue that the company should balance the interest of all stakeholders. For instance, Clarkson (1995) noted that 'the primary economic and social purpose of the corporation is to create and distribute increased wealth and values to all its primary stakeholder groups, without favouring one group at the expense of others'. Similarly, Jones and Wicks (1999) argue that 'the interests of all (legitimate) stakeholders have intrinsic value and no set of interests is assumed to dominate the others'.

Ethics and stakeholder concept have been examined from different perspectives. Donaldson and Preston's (1995) review of stakeholder literature found numerous explanations for, and application of, stakeholder theory: descriptive, instrumental and normative. The instrumental theory for instance links 'means' and 'ends' and advocates a causal relationship between organizational performance and the 'strategic management' of stakeholders. A fundamental assumption of the instrumental theory is that the ultimate objective of the firm is maximizing shareholder values and market success, and stakeholder management is a means to an end. Jones (1995) asserts that if a company contracts through its managers with its stakeholders on the basis of mutual trust and cooperation, they will have a competitive advantage over firms that do not. Beside the instrumental pre-scriptive approach to stakeholder management, few attempts have been made to describe how firms interact with stakeholders. Brenner and Cochran (1991) note that 'the stakeholder theory of the firm posits that the nature of an organization's stakeholders, their values, their relative influence on deci-sions and nature of the situation are well relevant information for predicting organizational behaviour'. Jones (1995) argues that ' managers behave as if stakeholders mattered because of the intrinsic justice of their stakeholders' claim on the firm'. Mitchell *et al.* (1997) have attempted to develop a 'descriptive stakeholder theory'. They propose certain attributes that con-tribute to the saliency of stakeholders. The central thesis of their stakeholder theory is that 'stakeholder salience will be positively related to the cumula-tive number of stakeholder attributes of power, legitimacy, and urgency' (Jawahar and McLaughlin 2001). According to Mitchell *et al.* (1997) it is the moral legitimacy of a stakeholder's claim, power to influence the firm, and the urgency of the stakeholder's issue that decide the saliency of the stake-holder and its importance to the firm. The Mitchell *et al.* (1997) model is crit-icized for focusing only on attributes that make a stakeholder salient, and ignores 'an issue central to stakeholder management: how an organization's management deals with stakeholders who vary in terms of salience' (Jawahar and McLaughlin 2001). Donaldson and Preston (1995) argue that the stakeholder theory is essentially normative and cannot be supported on descriptive and instrumental grounds alone.

The lion's share of management literature on the 'strategic' management of stakeholders is pragmatic, and takes a prudent approach (see Donaldson, 1999). The basic argument here is that for the firm to achieve its strategic objectives, stakeholders need to be considered because they have the potential to help or harm the firm in its quest to achieve its cor-porate objectives. The strategic management of stakeholders' approach looks for the best way to deal with primary stakeholders and powerful secondary stakeholders, whilst minimizing damage to shareholder value. It advocates the adoption of different approaches to deal with each primary stakeholder group according to certain attributes such as a degree of 'perceived' influence. Generally, the literature suggests a limited number of strategies including proaction, defence and reaction (Clarkson

1988, 1991, 1995). According to Clarkson and other earlier writers (e.g. Carroll 1979; Watrick and Cochran 1985) being proactive implies doing a great deal to address a stakeholder's issue, including 'anticipating and actively addressing specific concerns or leading an industry effort to do so' (Jawahar and McLaughlin 2001). Being proactive is to anticipate and fully accept one's responsibilities, being defensive is to admit responsibility but fight it, whilst reactives simply deny responsibility (Jawahar and McLaughlin 2001). An example of the proactive could be an organization involving the community or other primary stakeholder in the early discussion of a management plan such as (re)location, job cuts or expansion. The defence strategy involves doing only the minimum legally required by law to address a stakeholder's issue. This strategy involves a company preparing a defensive strategy for not going beyond what is legally required. The reactive strategy advises firms to involve either fighting against addressing a stakeholder's issue or completely withdrawing and ignoring the stakeholder (Jawahar and McLaughlin, 2001). An example of a defensive strategy would be Ford Motor Company's refusal to recall the Ford Pinto on the assumption that each explosion was an isolated incident (*Auto Week*, quoted in Jawahar and McLaughlin 2001). It must be noted that all four strategies are legally defensible, however, the first two strategies, although pragmatic strategies, are perhaps more satisfactory to stakeholders than the latter two strategies (defensive and reactive). According to the strategic literature, a firm should not opt for the first two because they are more satisfactory to stakeholders but they should do so when they *have* to, not because they *ought* to. For instance, according to the literature on the strategic management of stakeholders, if the defensive strategy is cheaper and less damaging to the firm (but damaging to a primary stakeholder) than a proactive strategy, then the firm should opt for the defensive strategy. The fundamental assumption here is that organizations operate in a highly competitive environment and have finite resources in terms of time and money, organizations are unlikely to (and they should not) proactively address and accommodate issues and concerns of all stakeholders all the time. Put differently, according to the strategic approach of stakeholder management, companies should only be proactive with stakeholders who hold power and have control over critical resources.

Donaldson and Preston (1995) list three different theoretical approaches to stakeholders: descriptive, instrumental and normative. The descriptive approach looks at whether stakeholder interests are taken into account or not; the instrumental approach, on the other hand, focuses primarily on the impact stakeholders may have, or not as the case may be, in terms of corporate effectiveness. And the normative approach is concerned with the reasons why corporations ought to consider stakeholder interests even in the absence of any apparent benefit (Gibson 2000).

The above discussion leads us to the question: is the strategic management of stakeholders ethical? There is no clear-cut answer. On the one hand, one could take a Kantian stand and argue that because the primary motive for dealing with stakeholder interests is to maximize shareholder values and thus lacks a moral component, and therefore it is less than truly moral and so unsound ethics. For instance Goodpaster and Holloran (1994) argued that 'strategic thinking leads to the elimination of ethics in favour of prudence'. On the other hand, according to the reconciliation thesis, firms can do good, even if it is based on self-interested acts, at the same time as they do well. Gibson (2000) noted that 'there is no necessary discontinuity between self-interest and morality, and that moral behaviour is consistent with rational prudence'. Gibson (2000) uses the platonic example (grounded in virtue theory) to illustrate his argument:

> The fact that many people restrain themselves from acting badly because of an abiding belief that they will be judged after death for their present actions. The truth of that belief need not be the issue, since the salient point is that a large proportion of the population act as it were true that their actions were subject to divine scrutiny.... It is entirely possible that Mother Teresa did her good works motivated by an unstated hope for heavenly rewards, yet this would make her no less saintly for many of her admirers.

Therefore, according to the reconciliation thesis, one should not automatically reject strategic management of stakeholders as amoral because there is a possibility that morality and pragmatism may often be coextensive (Gibson 2000). Goodpaster notes that 'once we understand that there is a practical "space" for identifying the ethical values shared by a corporation and its stockholders – a space that goes beyond strategic self-interest but stops short of impartiality – the hard work of filling that space can proceed' (quoted in Gibson 2000).

Another stream of literature asserts that organizations should properly look after stakeholder interests even if it is not profitable. Put differently, organizations should not ignore stakeholders in the absence of 'potential' benefit. This approach to stakeholders takes a deontological stand, and its basic thesis is that business should fulfil its *duties* towards primary and secondary stakeholders. In contrast to the pragmatic approach, the deontological approach looks at the moral motives rather than the outcome. Carroll (1993) notes that:

> To appreciate the concept of stakeholders, it helps to understand the idea of a stake. A stake is an interest or share in an undertaking... A stake is also a claim. A claim is an assertion to a title or a right to something (quoted in Gibson 2000).

Donaldson and Preston (1995) assert that:

Each group of stakeholder merits consideration for its own sake and not merely because of its ability to further the interests of some other groups, such as the shareowners.

Similarly, Evan and Freedman (1988) assert that stakeholder theory must be conceptualized 'along essentially Kantian lines', that is stakeholders must be treated as an end in themselves, and not as a mean to other ends such as maximizing shareholder value.

PRINCIPLES OF STAKEHOLDER MANAGEMENT

The Clarkson Centre for Business Ethics (2000) outlines the following core principles for stakeholder management:

- Principle 1 – Management should acknowledge and actively monitor the concerns of all legitimate stakeholders and should take their interests appropriately into account in decision making and operations.
- Principle 2 – Managers should listen to and openly communicate with stakeholders about their respective concerns and contributions, and about the risks that they assume because of their involvement with the corporation.
- Principle 3 – Managers should adopt processes and modes of behaviour that are sensitive to the concerns and capabilities of each stakeholder constituency.
- Principle 4 – Managers should recognize the interdependence of efforts and rewards among stakeholders, and should attempt to achieve a fair distribution of the benefits and burdens of corporate activity among them, taking into account their respective risks and vulnerabilities.
- Principle 5 – Managers should work cooperatively with other entities, both public and private, to ensure that risks and harms arising from corporate activities are minimized and, where they cannot be avoided, appropriately compensated.
- Principle 6 – Managers should avoid altogether activities that might jeopardize inalienable human rights (e.g. the right of life) or give rise to risks which, if clearly understood, would be patently unacceptable to relevant stakeholders.
- Principle 7 – Managers should acknowledge the potential conflicts between (a) their own role as corporate stakeholders, and (b) their legal and moral responsibilities for the interests of stakeholders, and should address such conflicts through open communication, appropriate reporting and incentive systems and, where necessary, third-party review.

SUMMARY

It appears that ethical behaviour, in the long run, may reduce the cost of social and economic partnership with different stakeholders. Corporate governance has become an increasingly pressing issue owing to the increasing separation of ownership from control, the sheer power of TNCs, and a recent rash of high-profile corporate failures. However, the practice of sound corporate governance is a complex business, needing considerable thought as to the most appropriate manner for reconciling divergent interests. Managers should take into consideration the rights of different groupings of shareholders, pay attention to disclosure and transparency, take into account the needs and interests of other groupings with an interest in the affairs of the firm, and seek to exercise objective judgement on corporate affairs. In this chapter we argued that, regardless of the primary intention of the company, good corporate governance and stakeholder management could enhance the company's long-term profit.

KEY QUESTIONS

1. Explain the reasons behind the increasing interest in the practice of corporate governance.
2. Do you think there can be a 'best practice' corporate governance model? Give reasons for your answer.
3. 'A stakeholder in an organization is any group or individual who can affect or is affected by the achievement of an organization's objectives'. Critically discuss this definition.
4. Outline and critically discuss the Clarkson Centre for Business Ethics' 'Core Principles for Stakeholder Management'.

CASE STUDY: TOWARDS SOCIAL ACCOUNTING?

'Rumblings that the (UK) Government is considering appointing a minister for corporate responsibility may signal a sea change in existing business philosophy, ushering in a new era of social accounting. Senior management and finance directors are coming under increasing pressure to throw out the rule book and look beyond wealth creation for the sake of wealth creation by taking up a more ethical stance.

It is a subject that is also being addressed as part of the continuing company law review. The Government is considering proposals that could result in a wider set of social accounting disclosure requirements being brought into UK law. The review has a hefty remit that covers a broad spectrum of issues, from poor payment practice to lack of community investment to trading with oppressive regimes.

According to Franceska van Dijk, senior consultant in SustainAbility, the strategic sustainable development consultancy, campaigners are lobbying for the introduction of the so-called triple bottom line. That is a set of accounts that stretches beyond financial reporting to cover social and environmental accounting, alongside economic measures.

Roger Adams, technical director of the Association of Chartered Certified Accountants (ACCA), says that thinktanks and non-governmental organisations, such as the New Economics Foundation and Amnesty International, are "increasingly putting companies under the spotlight".

High-profile public relations disasters include the Nike link to sweatshop labour in developing countries, and Monsanto's brush with the genetically modified foods backlash. However, it was Shell's necessary policy turnaround after Brent Spa in the mid-nineties that set the ball rolling.

Mr Adams says: "You are beginning to get this change in corporate thinking that it is no longer appropriate to try to bully the market by brand power. There is a realisation that even the strongest brand can be damaged if a company loses the trust of a particular group of stakeholders".

Because of this, a handful of global players, alongside a number of smaller firms, are trying to clean up their image. SustainAbility's clients include Ford, Shell, and Procter & Gamble, all of which, Ms van Dijk says "are very interested in the sustainable development debate and what it means for their business".

The push towards business with a conscience is far from altruistic. The argument that is likely to make finance directors sit up is that a body of opinion is forming that suggests that being a good corporate citizen adds value to a business, ultimately boosting the bottom line.

Resources are being put into identifying the business case. The World Business Council for Sustainable Development, a body of international companies committed to social accounting, last month released a report setting out why it makes business sense to adopt an ethical policy.' (*Times* 22/2/2000).

ISSUES

....

Do you think that – using the above case as an example – firms are acting ethically if their actions are purely prompted by financial concerns, but are likely to produce socially desirable results?

FURTHER READING

Freeman, R.E. 1984. *Strategic Management: A Stakeholder Approach*. Boston: Pitman. A path-breaking book. It examines strategic management from a stakeholder perspective.

Freeman, R.E. and Gilbert, D.R. Jr. 1988. *Corporate Strategy and the Search for Ethics*. Englewood Cliffs, NJ: Prentice-Hall. Discusses corporate governance, and a number of other pressing ethical issues in the context of strategic management.

Jones, T.M. 1995. 'Instrumental stakeholder theory: a synthesis of economics and ethics', *Academy of Management Review,* 20: 404–37. This article provides a good summary of stakeholder literature.

SOCIAL PARTNERSHIPS

Over the past decade, there has been increasing interest in the possibilities for social partnerships, especially ones that are characterized by deals between employers and employee representatives within a particular firm, or between the firm and community organizations. On the one hand, proponents of social partnerships have suggested that they represent the epitome of ethical management; firms are compromising their interests and making real concessions in order to improve the lot of the less endowed, be they individual employees or a disadvantaged community. On the other hand, critics of social partnerships have argued that their contemporary manifestations tend to be devoid of any moral worth; firms are motivated to enter into partnerships largely by the exigencies of profitability and to promote employee consent. In this chapter, we outline the changing nature and role of social partnerships, assess the relationship between classic corporate social responsibility and more recent partnership initiatives, outline current trends, and locate social partnerships within classical ethical theories.

WHAT IS A SOCIAL PARTNERSHIP?

As Guest (2001: 101) notes, partnership 'is one of those warm words, that can mean all things to all people'. Above all, partnership represents attempts to balance the needs of individuals (and communities) with those of the organization. As Prechel (1999) notes, 'successful social partnerships begin with acknowledging that there are legitimate partners within the workplace that have contrasting but legitimate interests: the firm and the economy'. Traditionally, social partnerships have been associated with what is referred to as the 'Rhineland model' implying long-term state support for representative trade unions, 'an affiliation to collective bargaining, and the establishment of long-term strategies between government, business and organized labour' (Beardwell and Holden 2001: 489; Iankova 1996). More recently, social partnerships have been taken to entail a recognition that, as members of an economic community, key stakeholders have a legitimate interest in an enterprise (see Chapter 2 for a fuller discussion of the concept of 'stakeholder').

Social responsibility represents 'the obligation a business assumes toward society…to be socially responsible is to maximize positive effects and minimize negative effects on society' (Ferrell *et al.* 2000: 6). Classic corporate social responsibility represents an attempt by the firm to divert a proportion of revenues to 'good to worthy causes, as well as finding creative ways to improve the quality of life of the firm's employees and the local community' (Ferrell *et al.* 2000: 278). However, any outreach is very much on the firm's terms; assistance is seen as a 'free gift' to be extended or revoked at will; the firm does what it sees as socially desirable, taking only limited account of the views and interests of the subject. Community-linked social partnerships are based on a recognition of the limits of classical corporate social responsibility initiatives; here the views of key stakeholders are considered and brought abroad, making for more sustainable and, ultimately successful out-reach initiatives.

As Rao and Sita (1993) note, 'the interactive relationship leading to mutual problem solving and benefits has been variably referred as a collab-orative or participative strategy', becoming a social partnership when issues and efforts of a broader scope are encompassed. Whilst much of the litera-ture on social partnerships focuses on possible long-term relations between unions and management (see Beardwell and Holden 2001; Guest 2001), social partnerships can also encompass deals reached between governments at central and local level, employers and communities (cf. Rao and Sita 1993). For example, a social partnership arrangement may develop between a multinational company and a host community to, say, reduce levels of environmental pollution. Similarly, a broadly based social partnership could provide community-based development organizations with the nec-essary resources and backing to 'undo the damage of business flight and racial animosity that plague poor communities' (Rubin 1993: 428). In short, social partnerships may be focused on the two central groupings within the firm, employers and employees – but with some degree of state involve-ment as well – or have a broader social focus, involving one or more com-munity groupings as well (Waddock and Post 1991). In Britain, much of the emphasis of contemporary literature has been on the former, in the United States the latter.

Social partnerships can only be realized through stakeholders making appropriate contributions for mutual benefit, which, in turn, is only poss-ible through an 'environment of relative equity and fairness' (Rubin 1993: 489). In short, what is sought is a situation of 'mutual advantage' (Huxham and Vangen 2000). Underpinning contemporary notions of a social partnership are a desire to provide some protection for individual employees and their collectives, but within a context that retains many of the key manifestations of the neo-liberal orthodoxy, including flexibility, general deregulation and an emphasis on ensuring competitiveness (Rubin 1993: 489).

Social partnerships are not necessarily characterized by an absence of conflict; rather, conflict becomes institutionalized, with established mecha-nisms for conflict resolution that do not endanger the existing social order (Kirichenko and Koudyukin 1993: 43). In other words, the emphasis of social partnerships is on fairness, inclusivity, economic growth and social progress rather than order at all costs.

To Waddock (1988), partnerships will only succeed if a degree of flexibil-ity is incorporated. In implementing a partnership, key issues include the anticipated fragility of any deal made, the time needed to develop a partner-ship, the degree of cooperation present, staff support, and the expectations of the various partners.

CLASSIC PARTNERSHIPS: BENEFITS AND COSTS

Corporatism refers to a particular type of political relationship in which the state includes interest groups directly in its decision-making bodies to promote class harmony and the common pursuit of national development and other goals. 'For corporatist regimes to be successful, an effective consensus or "social partnership" has to be forged, especially between employer and employee groups and organizations' (Marshall 1996). The pre-war variants of corporatism, as practised, for example, in Nazi German and fascist Italy, stressed the power of the state as the dominant party in decision making, the dependence of interest groups on state support, and their compulsory participation in public agencies. However, what is often referred to as neo-corporatism, as practised in Western Europe since the Second World War, emphasizes consensual decision making, independent interest group representation, their democratic control by members, and voluntary participation in the organs of the state. In the end, neo-corporatism seeks to promote greater stability and fairness within society (Breitenfellner 1997). Normally, such arrangements – which inevitably entail sacrificing short-term sectional interests for a long-term social gains – are only possible in a situation where there is a shared notion of crisis, and when there seem to be few viable alternatives. In other words, whilst neo-corporatism does entail a degree of altruism for long-term social gains, it seems that few are willing to espouse such an option unless they are effectively compelled to do so.

Indeed, it could be argued from a deontological standpoint, neo-corporatist deals are devoid of ethical worth, given that the underlying rationale may be that of necessity, rather than social betterment. However, some utilitarians would argue that *if* neo-corporatism can contribute to a fairer society, and, *if* in doing so, overall social prosperity and happiness is enhanced, neo-corporatism could indeed be seen as a more ethical policy option than an unfettered free market (albeit that neo-liberals would contest the functionality of corporatism in the first place).

Under neo-corporatism, wages and working conditions are not set by governments in authoritarian manner, or 'sacrificed to the cycle of markets'; rather they are regulated and stipulated by a sequence of deals and agreement (Kuhlmann 2000: 55). Wood and Harcourt (2001) argue that two elements of neo-corporatism are central:

> First, it is characterized by tripartism. The government discusses major economic problems, and how to solve them, with the employers and employees. Collective groups who engage in joint policy formulation represent interests. Although tripartism occurs at various levels (industry, national), consultations at the central level are another major characteristic of neo-corporatism (Corveers and van Veen 1995: 424). In short, neo-

corporatism is characterized as a centralized form of economic policy implementation, where co-ordination takes place neither through market forces nor via central diktat (Arestis and Marshall 1995: 8). Rather, the aim is to build consensus, compromise, and to promote mutual understanding, in short a 'negotiated economy', with central wage setting (ibid.: 8). However, the active participation of a broad range employers and unions is most likely to be secured if they will have to live with the results of any deal reached (Flanagan 1999: 1152).

A social or labour accord is a negotiated agreement between the main actors in the industrial relations domain (Maree 1995). It typically involves a package of measures based on trade-offs between the parties involved: 'It usually entails a package of measures or issues which the parties agree to in order to achieve the goals of the contract' (ibid.). Neo-corporatist countries are likely to have an essentially informal accord, whose origins often reflect the desire to promote greater social consensus and secure a more stable positive economic trajectory, particularly as noted earlier, in the absence of credible alternatives. Examples of countries that have experimented with non-authoritarian or neo-corporatism include Sweden and Austria.

Accords depend on organizations participating in neo-corporatist negotiations being sufficiently all encompassing, so that they cannot ignore the negative consequences of their actions (Crouch 1993: 9). In other words, if a collective achieves society-wider representation, however, it can no longer afford to ignore the wider social effects of what it does (ibid.: 50). This would be true for both unions and employer associations. In short, according to Olson's (1982) theory of encompassing organizations, labour accords become a viable means of pursuing the common social good *if* the partners to such a deal have a sufficiently broad 'social footprint'. Should a significant component of society find itself outside of the compass of an accord, it is likely that any deals will prove unsustainable. An example of this would be the Austrian case, where undynamic and increasingly corrupt political institutions led to the interests of increasingly narrow insider groupings being prioritized, contributing to the rise of a far right political party (see Casey and Gold 2000). More broadly speaking, critics of social accords have argued that the 'corporatist jobs machine' proved considerably less functional in the 1990s than hitherto (Sisson 1999: 17). Nonetheless, the question emerges as to whether the problems of neo-corporatism are simply one of degree; the problems associated with the Swedish case in particular, reflect specific institutional rigidities (Vartianen 1998: 19). Indeed, whilst there is little doubt that the Swedish system is relatively cumbersome, a broad consensus persists in a number of key areas, above all in terms of principles of redistribution (Vartianen 1998: 19).

Despite these limitations, it is evident that social accords can yield wide-ranging benefits in a number of areas, ranging from higher levels of social and infrastructural spending and lower social inequality, to a relatively stable growth trajectory and low levels of inflation. A contemporary accord could centre on union support for a controlled and gradual process of adjustment, a mutual recognition by unions and employers of each other's interests, and a greater respect for the capabilities and potential contributions of the other (Visser 1998: 289). Nonetheless, there is little doubt that neo-corporatism is considerably less fashionable in the early 2000s than hitherto; the ranks of corporatist countries has greatly thinned, with much of the contemporary literature on social partnerships focusing on more modest firm-centred deals (Wood and Harcourt 2000).

THE NEW SOCIAL PARTNERSHIPS: UNDERPINNINGS AND BENEFITS

Waddock (1988) argues that sound social partnerships will accrue meaningful benefits to all parties. Critical in the creation of partnerships is the existence of a problem that can only be solved through mutual interaction; 'including organizations and individuals holding a stake in the problem to be solved is central to partnership success' (Waddock 1988).

Successful social partnerships have often been upheld as one of the benefits of corporate success. However, much trumpeted partnership agreements have often failed to rescue companies from subsequent financial crises, good examples being Hyundai and Rover (Guest 2001: 103).

Whilst firmly committed to the neo-liberal policies of previous Conservative governments, the current Labour government in Britain has attempted to temper some of its worst excesses through promoting social partnerships. Certainly, this does not entail a return to the 'Rhineland model': indicative of this is that the word 'partnership' receives considerably more emphasis than the traditional term of 'social partnership' (Beardwell and Holden 2001: 489). What is envisaged is an emphasis on the mutual responsibilities of employers and employees, with unions and managers engaging in ongoing dialogue 'to introduce change, improve productivity and resolve disputes' (Beardwell and Holden 2001: 490). This desire is advocated in the Fairness of Work legislation, and through the 1999 Partnership Initiative, the latter providing some funding for new partnership arrangements (Guest 2001: 104).

Social partnerships have received broad backing from the British labour movement (Beardwell and Holden 2001: 490). Although this may simply reflect the vulnerability of unions, and the desire to retain some vestiges of support from the state and employers (Beardwell and Holden 2001: 490).

However, it can be argued that union members do have a strong interest in areas outside the traditional scope of collective bargaining; surveys of union members indicate that employees place a high premium on job security, quality of work and job fulfilment (Beardwell and Holden 2001: 490). Given this, it can be argued that unions have little option but to express support for social partnerships if they are to accurately represent the needs of their members. In the case of management, meaningful concessions will be necessary if any partnership deal is to get off the ground; management cannot endlessly repeat a stated commitment to partnership without, at the very least, broadening the scope of consultation.

Critics of the new social partnerships have argued that such deals are more likely to be motivated by the exigencies of profitability rather than fairness (cf. Breitenfellner 1997). Instead, social partnerships should centre on a broader social agenda, straddling national boundaries if need be. However, the latter is only likely to take place if labour unions are capable of coordinating their activities internationally, and through concerted action by individual national governments; essentially a form of super neo-corporatism would be the desired policy outcome (Breitenfellner 1997).

As noted earlier, new social partnerships need not necessarily focus on deals between employers and employee representatives; social partnerships may form part and parcel of corporate efforts at 'good citizenship' within the community. Such partnerships represent a more developed form of corporate social responsibility – not only does the firm simply 'do good works' in the community, but also acts in concert with community groupings to ensure that its outreach activities have maximum impact. For example, the revitalization of the urban centre of Cleveland in the United States in the late 1980s represented the outcome of ongoing partnerships between business and community organizations (Austin 1998). Proponents of such deals argue that a win–win situation is likely to result; again, overall social prosperity is promoted as well as a more attractive environment in which to do business. However, the rationale for such deals is again rather complex when viewed from a business ethics perspective; in entering such agreements are firms motivated by the desire for self-preservation and advancement, or by genuine moral concerns? Alternatively, it could be argued that community-linked social partnerships represent little more than a rewarmed version of classical corporate philanthropy – limited 'good works' done in order to make the relentless pursuit of profit more socially acceptable.

It could further be argued that many community-linked partnerships represent little more than a form of marketing by other means. Corporate assistance for community development may result in favourable exposure for the firm, both through formal and informal mechanisms. Again, partnerships to promote a green agenda – for example, alliances or linkages with

NGOs to promote or facilitate more environmentally sound production methods – may provide a ready opportunity to advertise a firm's green credentials. For example, critics have charged that US ice-cream firm, Ben and Jerry's social responsibility initiatives represented a cynical attempt through 'save the world marketing' through 'a series of feel-good stunts to sell high-price ice cream' (Ferrell *et al.* 2000: 280). However, many utilitarians would have little problem with such developments, as long as they result in a general bettering in the social condition, or, indeed, that of the biosphere.

An alternative, and somewhat bleaker view of corporate social responsibility – particularly in its more holistic partnership manifestations – is provided by David Korten. Korten asserts that, given the predatory nature of contemporary capitalism, with its emphasis on short-term profits, any company that acts in a socially responsible fashion is automatically placed at a weakness: 'corporate managers live and work in a system that is virtually feeding on the socially responsible' (quoted in Ferrell *et al.* 2000: 279).

Limits of social partnerships

As Guest (2001: 101) notes, the attraction of partnerships for unions include the fact that they represent one of the few viable routes through which they may be valued by employers, and yet still retain an independent voice. However, the cost entailed from any social partnership is that it may simply become a device for incorporation by management (Guest 2001: 101). Indeed, it can be argued that, 'despite its connotations of mutuality and mutual gains', it may in practice be weighted towards the company, with other partners contributing much more to the company's success than the company gives back to individual employees, collectives and communities (Guest 2001: 101). Employers may use partnerships as a means of pre-empting efforts by unions to broaden the scope of collective bargaining; if unions are ideologically committed to the notion of partnerships, they may be forced to accept a restriction on negotiation and the expansion of consultation (Beardwell and Holden 2001: 490).

Metcalf (1995) argues that, in Britain, traditional collective industrial relations 'is crumbling', possible outcomes being new forms of workplace-centred partnership, or authoritarian forms of workplace governance. However, whilst the former may result in greater productivity, they may undermine existing relationships between employers and unions that have been built up over many years.

Indeed, it is a common perception that practices often turn out to be primarily for the benefit of the company; what employees can do for the firm is given a far higher priority than what the firm can do for individuals or communities (Beardwell and Holden 2001: 101).

Moreover, there is considerable evidence to suggest that even those firms who might be expected 'to be on the leading edge of best practice' are still likely to be associated with low levels of trust, especially in terms of management trusting trade unions (Beardwell and Holden 2001: 101). Trust is only possible if all parties share a vision (Ferrell *et al.* 2000: 149). This has led Kelly (quoted in Beardwell and Holden 2001: 490) to argue that 'it is difficult, if not impossible to achieve a partnership with a party who would prefer that you didn't exist; the growth of employer hostility is a major objection to the case for union moderation'. In other words, given the strength of management and governmental ambivalence, there is little reason for employers to enter into truly meaningful partnerships, when they are capable of exercising their prerogative independently (Beardwell and Holden 2001: 490). Moreover, it can be argued that unions have had far more success in extracting genuine concessions from employers through traditional collective bargaining, especially when backed up with the threat of collective action from the shop floor (Beardwell and Holden 2001: 490).

Finally, despite the current Labour government's strong emphasis on 'partnership', it seems that partnership agreements – even those only directly involving employers and unions – have only gained a foothold at a small minority of British workplaces (Guest 2001: 102). Indeed, as Guest (2001: 103) notes, many partnerships seem to be borne out of a notion of crisis (just as was the case with the 'Rhineland model' partnerships). Partnership has indeed become institutionalized in Britain through various governmental initiatives, but these have yet to gain broader practical support (Guest 2001: 104); one of the few exceptions to this general rule being the Low Pay Commission (Metcalf 1999). Moreover, partnership only represents one of a plethora of alternative policy options open to the contemporary labour movement (see Hyman 1997).

Are social partnerships really ethical?

As Ferrell *et al.* (2000: 149) note, when the rights and interests of others are considered when decisions are made that affect them, higher levels of trust will be evident. Whilst, as noted earlier, even in 'best practice' cases, trust may be elusive, there is considerable evidence to suggest a generally ethical organizational environment and trust are closely associated (Ferrell *et al.* 2000: 149). Trust plays an important role 'in communicating ethical values and encouraging responsible conduct (Ferrell *et al.* 2000: 150). But, how is trust made? It is sometimes suggested that an established partnership arrangement will nurture higher levels of trust. However, it can be argued that trust is an extremely complex phenomenon; high levels of trust at the workplace are likely to be a product of a range of factors, of which a partnership arrangement may be simply one (cf. Mueller 1997).

SOCIAL PARTNERSHIPS AND EUROPEAN INTEGRATION

As Hyman (1997) notes, an important byproduct of social partnership debates have been efforts to introduce a social dialogue dimension into the process of European integration. It is argued that, in the age of increasingly mobile capital, it is desirable to strengthen transnational institutions, underpinned by international partnership agreements (Oberman 2000). Indeed, it can be argued that transnational partnership deals represent the best chance for preserving the classical 'Rhineland model' of social partnerships (Apeldoorn 2000). In the EU, social partnership has been promoted through a new article in the treaty, Article 118b, which prescribed that 'the Commission shall endeavour to develop the dialogue between management and labour at European level which could, if the two sides consider it desirable, lead to relations based on agreement', amplified in the Maastricht protocol (Hyman 1997). These agreements aim to promote agreements between management and labour at EU-wide level, agreements that could possibly become encoded in legislation. Critics have argued that, to date, this process has yielded little, other than placing considerable demands on trade union resources (Hyman 1997).

SOCIAL PARTNERSHIPS AND THE PHILOSOPHICAL TRADITION

A central theme of this volume has been whether, if solely motivated by the exigencies of profit, managerial decisions that ameliorate or enhance social conditions within or without the workplace, are devoid of any moral worth. A deontologist would argue that ethical decisions are only ethical if done for the right reasons; in contrast, a utilitarian would see any act that improves overall social happiness as essentially 'good'. This debate is of particular importance when social partnerships are considered; in most cases, viable social partnerships have only been established or reconstituted when there is a lack of viable policy alternatives and/or when managers see clear gains in terms of the 'bottom line'.

SUMMARY

Social partnerships are founded on the notion that the interests of management and labour are essentially heterogeneous; however, they may be reconciled through a series of deals and trade-offs (see Gebert and Boerner 1999). To proponents of such arrangements, the outcome of a successful social partnership is a 'win–win' situation, whereby the firm trades off genuine concessions calculated to improve the material circumstances of other parties in return for their support. To critics, in their contemporary manifestations, they represent little more than a crude attempt to build consent whilst firms ruthlessly seek to maximize profits, and, as such, are devoid of any moral worth. The social partnership debate underscores the complexity of the ethical dilemmas facing the modern firm; above all, the question as to why firms should act ethically in the first place. In other words, firms should consider whether ethical conduct is worth pursuing in its own right, or should be simply subordinated to the quest for profits.

KEY QUESTIONS

1. What, do you think, constitutes 'social partnerships'? Give reasons for your answer.
2. Discuss the benefits and limitations of the 'classic social partnerships' associated with the practice of neo-corporatism.
3. Introduce and critically discuss the new social partnerships promoted by New Labour in Britain.

CASE STUDY: PARTNERSHIP AGREEMENTS: DAIMLER-CHRYSLER SOUTH AFRICA

During the apartheid era, South Africa had a closed economy, characterized by high levels of state intervention. Shielded by high protective tariff walls, and assisted by state incentives, a significant motor industry developed, moving beyond the mere assembly of knockdown kits to the manufacture of complete vehicles containing a large proportion of locally manufactured components. During the apartheid years, the company, then known as Daimler-Benz South

Africa gained a reputation for superior wage levels when compared to the rest of the South African motor industry and significant levels of social outreach expenditure, ranging from funding for sports activities to the beautification of the physical environment around the firm's East London manufacturing plant. Critics charged that this represented little more than 'guilt money', given the firm's refusal to join North American motor firms that had disinvested from South Africa as a means of protesting against apartheid – and the fact that at various stages, it supplied truck components ultimately used by the South African military. The firm was also plagued by high levels of workplace militancy culminating in a protracted strike/factory occupation that took place in 1990. The striking workers were opposed to the introduction of centralized bargaining in the motor industry, given that the firm offered considerably better conditions of service than other employers in the industry. The factory occupation was opposed by a significant component of the workforce, however, and the strikers were dismissed as a result of their actions.

The ending of apartheid also brought with it the phasing out of protective tariffs and reduced levels of state intervention in the economy; in response to pressure from global financial institutions, the ruling African National Congress's economic policies are largely neo-liberal in character. In the case of the motor industry, however, an imaginative deal between the government and the main players in the industry has resulted in the phased reduction of tariff barriers. Manufacturers can now import components in return for an equal value of exports. This has led to several motor manufacturers gearing up production for the world markets; Daimler-Benz South Africa (now known as Daimler-Chrysler South Africa) concentrating on exports of C-class motor cars. However, export contracts were contingent on meeting rigorous cost, productivity and quality criteria set by the parent company.

This led to management negotiating a partnership agreement, a deal being reached in mid-2001. To management, this agreement was primarily aimed at ensuring high quality and timely deliveries following the winning of major export orders. The incentive plan would enable workers to take home up to 23.5 weeks extra wages a year. The deals also allowed for draws for consumer goods; participation in the draws being contingent on high levels of attendance. However, shortly after the deal was struck a major nation-wide strike broke out across the South African motor industry, over wages. The strike was characterized by bitter exchanges between Daimler-Chrysler management and union officials as to what a partnership deal was really about. To managers, the strike was a violation of the spirit of the deal; to the union, the deal was simply a limited trade-off, which did not free management from their obligation to pay a 'living wage'. Eventually, the strike was resolved through a pay compromise.

This dispute highlighted the fact that partnership agreements do not necessarily reflect the main parties sharing basic goals and values.

ISSUES

Do you think that modern social partnerships represent a reflection of more ethical managerial strategies or simply a tool for enhancing profits? In other words, are they simply there to ensure greater productivity, or should they represent the outcome of genuine concessions and trade-offs and explicitly aim to ensure greater fairness at the workplace and/or within wider society?

FURTHER READING

Austin, J. 1998 'Business leadership lessons from the Cleveland turnaround', *California Management Review*, 41, 1: 86–106. An interesting account of how close community relations may yield unexpected dividends.

Casey, B. and Gold, M. 2000. *Social Partnerships and Economic Performance*. Cheltenham: Edward Elgar. A detailed assessment of the effectiveness of the traditional West European approach to social partnerships.

Guest, D. 2001. 'Industrial relations and human resource management', Storey, J. (ed.), *Human Resource Management*. London: Thomson Learning. An interesting overview; includes an assessment of new trends in social partnerships.

ENVIRONMENTAL ISSUES

The environment is often not cast as an ethical issue at all, but something which firms should take account of to secure their long-term profitability. Nonetheless, there is little doubt that environmental debates are fundamentally ethical ones. In this chapter, we explore the relationship between business and the environment, both in terms of theoretical debates and contemporary issues.

WHAT IS ENVIRONMENTAL ETHICS?

The environment can be defined as 'a dynamic and evolving system of natural and human factors in which all living organisms operate or human activities take place, and what has an direct or indirect...effect or influence on human actions at a given time in a circumscribed area (Vaillancourt, in Kulkarni 2000). Environmental ethics aims to provide ethical guidelines governing humanity's relationship with nature. A green firm will adopt 'resource conservation and environmentally friendly strategies at all stages of the value chain' (Oyewole 2001).

A number of writers in the fields of business and environmental ethics have argued that the firm needs to meet the concerns of all relevant stakeholders regarding the environment (Kulkarni 2000). However, particularly if different stakeholder groupings have different agendas, disputes may arise, with the exigencies of short-term wealth creation overriding long-term environmental concerns, leading to calls for a fairer negotiating framework founded on trust (Kulkarni 2000).

There is little doubt that trust matters – not just with regard to the environment, but also with a wide range of other ethical issues. The importance of firms being able to operate in an environment of trust is underscored by the proliferation of ethical codes of conduct, aimed at setting yardsticks to be adhered to, and rules governing disclosure of information (Kulkarni 2000).

WHY DOES THE ENVIRONMENT MATTER?

There is a range of reasons why firms should take the environment seriously. First, it has been argued, quite simply, that wilful environmental devastation is ruining the planet; it is becoming increasingly obvious that 'what goes around goes around' (Graybill 2000; Welford 1995). An increasingly visible example of the latter would be global warming. It has now been widely recognized that excessive emissions of carbon dioxide and other greenhouse gasses from industry and intensive farming have already had adverse consequences for the global climate, and that a 60 per cent reduction in carbon dioxide emissions will be necessary to stabilize atmospheric concentration (Roberts and Sheail 1993). This has led to a number of major industrial countries to take concrete steps to control the scale of atmospheric

51

pollution. Unfortunately, the world's largest producer of greenhouse gasses, the United States, remains reluctant to take serious measures in this regard.

Secondly, there is the legal dimension. There has been a great proliferation of environmental legislation (Rezaee 2000). Environmental issues are increasingly popular with both politicians and the wider community (Anonymous 2000). There is always an incentive for firms to resort to free riding, to try and opt out from any limiting ground rules, no matter how ethically desirable. However, the proliferation of environmental legislation has greatly constrained the ability of firms to do so (Welford 1995: 10).

Moreover, looking after the environment increasingly makes economic sense. There is a strong demand for green products. Whilst this is especially the case in Western Europe (for example, opinion surveys have indicated that 80 per cent of consumers in Germany, Italy and Spain would switch to greener products if given the opportunity), this demand is rapidly spreading worldwide (Oyewole 2001). People are inherently risk-adverse; they will choose greener products if there is a fear of the personal health costs of 'ungreen' goods (Oyewole 2001). However, it should be noted that this risk aversion varies greatly between social contexts. For example, in the United States, consumers have been far more willing to accept genetically modified foods than in Europe. In addition, there is the question as to how much more consumers are willing to pay for green products; a common argument is that the polluters should pay for the consequences of their actions, yet, of course, unclean industries are ultimately a product of consumer demand (Wyburd 1993).

Traditionally firms have viewed meeting environmental concerns simply as a cost. For example, the American Petroleum Institute has argued that conservation measures cost 400 000 jobs in the oil industry in the 1980s (Kulkarni 2000) (of course, this argument does not take account of jobs that may have been generated in alternative energy production, and in monitoring or pollution reduction equipment). However, as noted earlier, it has become 'good business' for firms to take the environment seriously, which would include the promotion of products which reduce waste and use energy more efficiently. In the marketplace, firms have to flexibly respond to consumer pressures. (Welford 1995: 11). Whilst critics have charged that 'green marketing' is often characterized by overstatement, there is little doubt that there are plenty of pressure groups and competitors willing to expose others' false claims (Welford 1995: 45).

The need for greater environmental concern is eroded by the tendency of firms to focus on short-term profits; however, it has become increasingly clear that firms may pay a heavy premium for this in terms of loss of trust by the community (Oyewole 2001). It can be argued that the wasteful use of resources reflects an organizational culture of expediency and indifference, hardly conducive to promoting customer loyalty (Welford 1995: 40). A loss of trust may result in debilitating conflicts between the firm, and community organizations and regulatory agencies, with considerable attendant costs (Welford 1995). Should the firm lack legitimacy, its future survival becomes questionable (Bansal and Roth 2000). In contrast, a high trust environment may be a valuable basis for rent generation over the long term. Firms are coming under considerable social pressure to be seen as 'good environmental citizens' in terms of overall environmental policies (Rezaee 2000).

There is little doubt that public opinion has become a powerful force in encouraging firms to take environmental issues seriously. Often cited examples would include Shell being forced to back track over the Brent Spar oil platform and the conspicuous success of explicitly green firms such as The Body Shop. However, whilst there is little doubt that public opinion does matter, consumers and the community tend to have far less information at their disposal than the firm. The latter will automatically have far more knowledge about the nature of the products they produce, the raw materials required, the process employed, and the wastes generated (Kulkarni 2000). Short-term profit maximization may make it desirable to conceal as much information as possible from the community, especially if large-scale environmental shortcuts are employed. Firms may be reluctant to impart information so as not to give competitors an edge, as well as for simply opportunism (Kulkarni 2000). In other words, an information asymmetry may encourage the firm to ignore environmental concerns (Andrews 2000). 'Dirty industries' such as mining and oil have tended to form close-knit industry associations, working within peer groups; strong pressures mitigate against being environmentally innovative, so as not to 'ratchet up standards for other' (Bansal and Roth 2000). As one oil manager remarked, 'the closer you get to the marketplace, the more careful you must be what you disclose' (quoted in Bansal and Roth 2000).

Moreover, firms are particularly likely to pollute poorer communities, where people may have less knowledge, and be less likely to object (Kulkarni 2000). For example in the United States, three out of five African and Hispanic communities live close to uncontrolled toxic waste sites (Oyewole 2001). Meanwhile, the export of toxic waste to the third world has become a lucrative business. This issue is dealt with more fully in the following chapter. These issues have led to calls for more rigid disclosure requirements, to level the playing field between firms and society at large (Andrews 2000). Oyewole (2001) has suggested that it is critical that environmental justice be secured. This would entail fairness in environmental practices, without discrimination on the grounds of gender or race.

The increasing pressures on firms to be more environmentally responsible has led to increasing interest in environmental audits and standardized environmental management systems, with the objective of achieving fixed environmental yardsticks, and greater transparency (Fussel and George 2000). Although this has been primarily associated with industry, it has gradually spread to the service sector (Fussel and George 2000). However, there is little doubt that the question as to what constitutes environmental 'best practice' remains a highly contentious one, and varies greatly from social context to social context. Moreover, whilst many firms seek to develop comprehensive strategies for dealing with environmental issues, others will do the bare minimum to avoid 'trouble' with regulatory agencies or social pressure groups (Bansal and Roth 2000). In other words, firms may simply seek to appease powerful stakeholder groups, or be environmentally responsible in order to realize notions of obligation, or as part-and-parcel of meeting some broader philanthropic agenda. The latter would entail doing the 'right thing' for 'feel good' or moral reasons (Bansal and Roth 2000).

POLICY ISSUES AND PRESSURES

In determining environmental policies, firms are not only subject to consumer and social pressures, but also the nature of the products and waste produced, their specific demands on raw materials, their geographical locale, industrial sector, and state regulations (Andrews 2000).

As a result, the approaches firms adopt towards the environment are often fragmented and reactive. Moreover, an atmosphere of confrontationalism between the state, firms and social actors may preclude the engendering of new synergies and the building of a collective future based on mutual understanding (Andrews 2000). This has led to writers such as Kleindorfer to suggest that more appropriate institutional contexts need to be developed, where environmental issues may be debated and tackled in a more constructive and holistic fashion (Andrews 2000).

An alternative argument is that firms need to be more proactive; in developing environmental policies, the 'hand of management' should be visible, rather than ad-hoc reactions to the 'hand of government' (Kulkarni 2000). In other words, it can be argued that firms need to be more proactive in developing strategic self-regulatory mechanisms, rather than being prisoners of external demands (Maxwell, Lyon and Hackett 2000; Meyer 2000). As writers such as Goodpaster have argued, firms do have an interest in the welfare of society, particularly in terms of securing a long-term role (Kulkarni 2000). Indeed, it can be argued that an enterprise strategy, which integrates the moral responsibilities of a firm into a clear vision as a basis for managerial policies and actions, should be extended to encompass ecological concerns (Stead and Stead 2000). In other words, the ethical roots of what a firms stands for should be broadened to encompass environmental concerns (Stead and Stead 2000).

It should be recognized that greening is a contested domain and open to multiple interpretations. As a result, environmental policies are inevitably 'contingent, local and variable' (Fussel and George 2000). Many firms will simply concentrate on areas that are highly visible and where the benefits can be clearly measured, such as energy-saving initiatives, whilst steering clear from more complex policies that could adversely affect profitability (Meyer 2000).

ENVIRONMENTAL PRACTICES

Whilst there has been greater use of recycling techniques, many recyclable goods continue to be disposed of by other means, most notably in the world's largest economy, the United States. On the one hand, it can be argued that recycling ultimately makes economic sense, and that, particularly at the collection and initial processing stages, the recycling business is both lucrative and labour intensive (Alexander 2000). On the other hand, this fails to answer the question as to why so many apparently recyclable goods are disposed of by other means. In practice, recycling certain products – steel, certain types of plastic and paper – are particularly profitable – and others less so – whilst landfill disposal remains a cheap and convenient alternative (Goldstein and Madtes 2000). This has led to arguments that landfill is artificially cheap – if the long-term environmental costs are considered – and recycling is not being properly costed in terms of the benefits it accrues. Currently, the United States only recycles 33 per cent of all goods; whilst this percentage is very slowly increasing, outright waste disposal remains an economical alternative (Goldstein and Madtes 2000).

This has led to suggestions that the scope of producer responsibility should be extended to encompass what happens to a product during its life cycle (Bellman and Khare 2000). It is argued that this can be achieved through market-orientated costing and support, and for greater transparency at economic and technical levels. In other words, products need to be more realistically costed, including costs of final disposal or recycling. This should be factored into pricing, in return for the producer taking care of the expenses associated with disposal or reuse. This would result in a more realistic – and ultimately more lucrative – market for recycling, whilst both producers and consumers would become aware of the real costs of using particular products (Bellman and Khare 2000). However, if consumers are prepared to pay more for green products – and, in many areas, they palpably are – the potential exists for a win–win situation, with green firms securing continued profits, and the environment being protected (Oyewole 2001).

Indeed, a number of prominent firms, most notably within the European motor industry, have already assumed some responsibility for their products throughout their life cycles; however, they remain a small minority.

Another increasingly contentious issue is the use of animals in experiments and in intensive farming. The question of humanity's treatment of animals is a long-standing one. Charles Darwin highlighted the close evolutionary connection between people and animals, and on account of this, was highly critical of the high prevalence of deliberate cruelty towards animals (*Evening Standard* 16/1/2001). Peter Singer has pointed out that a large proportion animal experiments are unnecessary; for example, there is already a vast range of cosmetics available which are proven to be harmless to people; thus, further testing of cosmetics on animals is unethical (Singer 1995: 66). Similarly, other experiments are often repeated ad nauseum. For example, H.F. Harlow of the Primate Research Center in the United States proved that if reared in conditions of maternal deprivation and isolation, rhesus monkeys could be reduced to a state of persistent depression or fear; these experiments – whose outcome may seem obvious – were repeated over a 15-year period, and continue to be after his death (Singer 1995: 66). The benefits of the experiments – and similar research – is arguably slight or non-existent (Singer 1995: 66); the interests of non-human beings are totally ignored (Singer 1995: 67). Moreover, recent research has shown that the differences between people and animals are less absolute than previously believed. Not only is there evidence that animals do form social communities of their own, but the DNA of the great apes is 98 per cent similar to that of people (*Financial Times* 20/2/2001). Moreover, a number of gorillas and chimpanzees have been successfully taught the sign language employed by deaf humans and show evidence of relatively advanced consciousness and memory (Singer 1995: 74). Singer argues that ethical conduct does not mean we discard partiality or personal relationships, but rather that we should be able to see the moral claims of those affected by our actions with 'some degree of independence from our feelings for them', be they people or other animals (Singer 1995: 77). It can, of course, be argued that the battle against animal experiments is partially over; most Western governments have greatly restricted the scale and scope of animal experimentation, but certainly experimentation continues on a large scale.

In the United Kingdom, Huntingdon Life Sciences, which routinely engages in animal experiments, has been driven to the brink of bankruptcy by protests against its staffers and financial backers. Investors have increasingly been cautious about firms conspicuously engaging in animal experimentation; it is a line of business which is no longer as profitable as hitherto (*Financial Times* 16/2/2001). Again, however, it could be argued that such decisions are devoid of any moral worth, if they are solely motivated by concerns as to loss of profits, rather than the wellbeing of the animals involved.

Scientists involved in animal experimentation have often claimed that they are being unfairly subjected to public scrutiny, given that the scale of animal suffering in the farming industry is very much worse; some 2.5 million animals a year in Britain are subject to experiments, compared to some 700 million who are slaughtered for the meat industry (*Financial*

Times 20/2/2001). However, it could be argued that this does not make a lesser evil any more desirable.

Singer points out that edible crops produce a far higher food value than livestock farming; if grains are fed to animals, only 10 per cent of the nutritional value is transferred to the resultant meat (Singer 1995: 63). In the West, excessive amounts of meat are consumed as a luxury item when alternatives are available. This has led Singer to pose the question in utilitarian terms: can a minor interest of those living in the advanced societies, be reconciled with the major interest of those in the developing world who do not have access to enough food or the sufferings of the animals involved (Singer 1995: 63)? In other words, intensive meat farming is unnecessarily wasteful, especially given food shortages in large areas of the developing world: 38 per cent of the earth's grain crop is fed to livestock. In addition, livestock farming has led to the clearing of large areas of rain forest in Central and South America (Singer 1995: 288). Moreover, factory farming is not just an issue of animal welfare; it has also led to pollution – intensive cattle farming, for example, is a major source of methane and other greenhouse gases – the depopulation of the countryside, and serious health problems (Harrison 1993). However, it is only recently that the meat industry has come under popular scrutiny as a result of repeated health scares, ranging from salmonella outbreaks traceable to battery farmed chicken to the BSE epidemic.

Again, however, it can be argued that mounting public pressure for changes in farming methods is a profoundly amoral process in that it is primarily prompted by the immediate personal health concerns of consumers, rather than a concern for the environment or the animals involved. Organic farming has proved increasingly lucrative, whilst Sweden meat exports have boomed as a result of the legal abolition of factory farming in that country. However, utilitarians such as Singer (1995) have argued that such debates are of little practical value; whatever the motivation, any reduction in overall suffering is desirable. Nonetheless, even if one operated from premise that the 'infliction of suffering on animals (should be prohibited) only when the interests of humans will be affected to anything like the extent that animals are affected', important changes would be necessary in society: new attitudes to wildlife and hunting for recreation, the trapping and wearing of furs, farming methods, and the range and choice of goods available (Singer 1995).

Finally, whilst it is easy – and potentially lucrative – for firms to claim sound environmental policies, there are a wide range of manners in which this may be measured (Wilks 2000). For example, it could be claimed that a timber product is from sustainable plantations, when, as noted in Chapter 1, this may have entailed the destruction of indigenous forests and/or the devastation of river systems. However, there is increasing pressure for global standards. In 1996, the International Organization for Standardization developed the ISO 14000 criteria (Rezaeee 2000). This provides voluntary guidelines for environmental management and auditing, and already has proven popular with commercial firms hoping to keep one step ahead of governmental regulation (see Rezaeee 2000).

PHILOSOPHY AND THE ENVIRONMENT

Both the Judeo-Christian tradition and classical philosophy place 'man' at the apex of creation, with a strong focus on the needs of present generations (Singer 1995: 269; Aristotle 1952). However, even within this tradition, it can be argued that some conservation is necessary. For example, the wellbeing of present generations of humanity may be threatened by the effects of ozone depletion. Similarly, the 'remnants of true wilderness are left to us like islands amidst a sea of human activity that threatens to engulf them'; the wilderness has a strong scarcity value which cannot be discounted (Singer 1995: 269). It is very difficult to calculate the long-term cost of loss of, say, an entire forest; certainly this more than just an aesthetic loss. It can be argued that a certain weighting should be given to the value of preserving an ecosystem for its own intrinsic worth, in addition to the undoubted scientific, recreational and economic benefits that may accrue to humans in the future (Singer 1995: 276).

Neo-liberals have deployed the classic utilitarian vision to see firms as purely orientated towards growth and material accumulation (Crane 2000a). If consumers are concerned about the environmental effects or health implications of a product, they will cease to buy it; 'good behaviour' is rewarded by the 'invisible hand of the market' (Browne and Kubasek 2001). However, this assumes that consumers will have perfect knowledge, and that markets are truly functional, when in the real word, neither is the case (Browne and Kubasek 2001). Moreover, it can be argued that this vision is rather misplaced in the context of palpably finite resources, and pan-global and transgenerational pollution (Browne and Kubasek 2001). Welford (1995: 5) argues that unrestrained free markets have failed to bring about equitable distributions of income, to protect the third world, and have done little to protect the planet. Indeed, the capacity of the environment to supply raw materials and assimilate waste, whilst maintaining bio-diversity and the overall quality of life is being increasingly undermined (Welford 1995: 6).

In Western society, there persists a strong emphasis on present, and short-termism (Singer 1995: 270). Neo-classical economics tends to discount future value (Singer 1995: 271) However, some things, when destroyed are lost forever; a loss may be incalculable, when the interests of not one, but many future generations are considered (Singer 1995). For example, many dams will last only a couple of generations before silting up, yet inflict permanent damage on river systems, coastlines and, indeed long-term agricultural potential. Singer (1995: 272) argues that even if the possible future material benefits accruing from conservation are discounted, the generations to come should be left with the right to choose if, for example, they wish to gain fulfilment through spending time in wilderness areas (Singer 1995: 272). Contemporary utilitarian theorist, Peter Singer, argues for a modification of the classic utilitarian view to take more accurate account of the future, as adverse to the present, immediate effects of actions. Singer argues the interests of non-human sentient beings and future generations of humanity have particular rights which should also be taken account of (Singer 1995: 286).

Recently, there have also been efforts to apply Rousseau's theory of the social contract to environmental issues. For example, Donaldson's social contract theory of business holds that whilst business benefits from – and, indeed depends for its survival on – wider society, this does entail some necessary costs (Oyewole 2001). Above all, firms must enhance the welfare of society, and adhere to basic standards of justice, including environmental justice. Whilst some costs will be passed on to the consumers in terms of higher prices, this will be considerably less than the costs of 'environmental victimization'. The latter would include increased diseases, birth defects and inhuman living conditions; these are 'costs with negative results' (Oyewole 2001). In contrast, greening will inevitably entail some costs too, but these would be 'costs with positive results', being beneficial to both the firm and the community in the long term (Oyewole 2001).

Others have argued that it is necessary to get beyond a 'homocentric' or 'speciesist' view that it is acceptable to damage the environment, as long as the people most immediately affected are compensated (Hoffman 1997: 236). Up until the nineteenth century, it was commonly held that it was justifiable to deny slaves basic human rights (Singer 1995: 60). Well into the 1950s, significant numbers of mentally impaired humans and/or the very poor were subject to laboratory experiments and/or enforced sterilization in many of the advanced societies. Today, it is increasingly accepted that certain forms of conduct may be ethically unacceptable, even if a human being is not at the receiving end (Singer 1995: 60). Mammals clearly have capacity to feel pain, a capacity for suffering, although this may vary from species to species, and, it has been argued that with this comes certain inherent rights, even if, at times, difficult trade-offs may be necessary (Singer 1995: 59; Welford 1995).

THE HARD GREEN PERSPECTIVE

The hard green perspective has tended to depict itself as the 'free market' approach to the environment. Indeed, there are certain parallels between this approach and the vision of neo-liberal theorists such as Milton Friedman

(1997), who have stressed the prosperity of the firm as providing the ulti-mate basis for general prosperity and progress. Neo-liberals would argue the firm has no moral obligations other than to its shareholders, yet, through the relentless pursuit of profits – and sensitivity to market forces – environ-mental issues will come on the agenda should and when wastage becomes overly costly or consumers prove reluctant to buy ungreen products.

Similarly, hard green writers such as Peter Huber have suggested that conservation should only be based on the incentives and signals from the market (Jackson 2001). Environmental issues are the natural preserve of con-servatives who should be concerned with environmental issues within a broader agenda to promote 'progress'. Huber argues that, for example, the use of high yield pest resistant crops will reduce demands on land, whilst nuclear energy is resource-efficient; it is necessary to place environmental issues in proper perspective (Jackson 2001). The problem with this vision is, of course, that it is somewhat incomplete; for example, it is not just a ques-tion of what kind of seeds are grown, but what kind of crops are produced, and whether they will be utilized in an wasteful way or not.

To Huber, environmental ethics should be firmly placed within the Judeo-Christian tradition; people should be put first under all circum-stances (quoted in Jackson 2001). The aesthetic value of the environment should be balanced against the needs of firms to pursue profits and the immediate needs of people (quoted in Jackson 2001). Interestingly, in common with radical environmental activists, the hard environmental per-spective is very suspicious of the role of science. Huber argues that envi-ronmental concerns – such as global warming – are the product of 'abstract computer models', which do not take account of the necessity for private gain and human welfare (Jackson 2001). Huber's condemnation of such 'pagan' science and his religious absolutism stands in stark contrast not only to more progressive environmentalism, but also to business people and commentators who have promoted environmental concerns for prag-matic reasons.

THE DEEP ECOLOGY PERSPECTIVE

To deep ecologists, it is only possible to have 'zero adverse effect' on the environment – or as little as possible – if there is a complete moral transfor-mation within the firm (and society) and the elevation of environmental goals above the exigencies of profitability (Crane 2000). It is virtually impos-sible to calculate in financial terms the loss, say of an entire forest, not just in aesthetic terms, but as a distinct ecosystem. Deep ecology argues that the value of entire natural communities in terms of species diversity – and as a functioning whole cannot be discounted (Singer 1995: 276).

Deep ecology sees the community as consisting not just of people, but also the physical environment around it – a 'land ethic' encompassing people, animals, plants, soil, water, or collectively, 'the land' (Singer 1995: 280). This is based on the assumption that all forms of life have some or other value in themselves, irrespective of use to humans. This includes the overall diversity of life; humans have no right to reduce this diversity other than meeting their vital needs (Singer 1995: 281). A limitation of the 'deep ecology' viewpoint is gauging the worth of inanimate things, of entire ecosystems (Singer 1995: 284).

It can be argued that existing reformist efforts have been proven inadequate in staving off a mounting crisis and that more radical measures are needed (Welford 1995: 2). Too often, the approach adopted is one of 'business as usual' supplemented by marginal changes when the negative effects of environmental degradation are glaringly obvious (Welford 1995: 2). Welford (1995: 3) argues that it should be recognized that economic activity is only part of wider processes that sustain life on earth. Whilst the 'green revolution' involving the widespread use of new strains of seeds and fertilizer resulted in increasing food production in the 1960s and 1970s, it has become increasingly obvious that the faith in the technological fixes is overstated (Welford 1995). This would include the loss of hardy native crops, 'sick plants who cannot withstand pests' without extensive use of fertilizers, erosion and water contaminated by pesticides (Welford 1995: 4). There is still insufficient evidence to conclude that the widespread introduction of genetically modified crops will be more beneficial than detrimental to humanity.

Welford (1995: 4) argues that, whilst it is hard for firms to refute the general need for environmental protection, it is considerably easier to respond in a piecemeal way with 'bolt-on strategies', in order to avoid having to face up to real challenges. There is little doubt that, for example, there has been substantial climatic change through human activity. This has led some writers to argue that 'we live in a post-natural world…we have crossed a threshold in the development of the planet'; the environment has already been irreparably damaged, and it is vital to conserve what is remaining (McKibben quoted in Singer 1995: 273). In contrast, to the traditional focus of profits, there is a need for organizations to become 'transcendent', treating green issues as paramount, seeing people as not above, but as one with nature, environmental values as being associated with sustainable development and long-term survival (Welford 1995: 193).

The deep ecology perspective has traditionally been unpopular with firms; it comes with the attendant baggage of being seen as associated with the 'beads and bangles brigade'. Even if managers may sympathize with much of the deep ecology vision, they are often to keen to couch environmental concerns within the discourse of securing long-term profitability (see Crane 2000). On the one hand, it could be argued that the deep ecology perspective needs to become more business friendly; as it stands, it argues that a fundamental moral overhaul is necessary, and that ecological problems can only be fully resolved through non-market solutions. Moreover, it can be suggested that it is overly prescriptive, without properly exploring what underlies the decision of firms to go green. On the other hand, it could be suggested that if environmental concerns are simply reduced to cost-benefit issues, the broader ecological picture may become blurred. (Crane 2000). Indeed, it could be argued that deep ecology provides a much-needed moral high ground, even if firms have to operate within an atmosphere of compromise. Moreover, whilst some of what the deep ecologists have to say remains at the fringes of environmental discourse, many of their ideas have now entered the generally accepted 'mainstream' (cf. Welford 1995). Increasingly, it is recognized that the world is a place where people dwell, rather than a 'preconstituted base for human action' (Attfield 1999: 11; Weschler 1999).

The need for more practical tools in the real world has led Peter Singer to argue that, given that people face a vast threat to their survival as a result of their destruction of the environment, any action that results in further destruction of the environment is ethically dubious, that which is unnecessarily harmful is patently wrong. To Singer, ecologically insensitive actions, such as carelessly throwing out waste that can be recycled is vandalism, and little more than the theft of 'our common property' of the earth's resources.

THE 'MIDDLE GROUND'

It is often argued that environmental issues are necessarily at odds with the logic of capitalism (Prothero and Fitchett 2000). Struggles between firms and environmental activists are seen as David and Goliath struggles, examples being the McLibel case (regarding McDonald's food products) and Greenpeace vs. Shell. Invariably, this results in the mighty being humbled, or a new martyr being created (Prothero and Fitchett 2000). In contrast to these arguments – and those of hard green theorists – there have been attempts to develop a more pragmatic perspective, allowing for more 'realistic' compromises than would be suggested by the hard green or deep ecology visions. It is argued that environmental problems are the inevitable result of development, and that some trade-offs are inevitable. This would entail both changes in consumer attitudes – an even greater awareness of the importance and implications of buying green – and that held by managers – an acceptance that a narrow focus on profits may be detrimental in the medium and long term (Prothero and Fitchett 2000).

In contrast to minimalist definitions of greening which would entail measures such as add-on pollution control, or perhaps basic environmental auditing, middle-ground approaches would entail auditing for sustainability and/or the firm taking responsibility for all stages of the product's life from raw materials to ensuring its recyclability. However, this would fall short of deep ecology arguments for fundamental economic and social change (Welford 1995).

Organizations need to see their survival and continued prosperity in the context of the exigencies of securing sustainability. There is a need to strike a balance between economic success and ecological protection, whilst it should be recognized that the two are not necessarily mutually reinforcing under all circumstances (Stead and Stead 2000). The 'compromise perspective' is still an emerging one; it lacks the clear focus of the hard green and deep ecology alternatives. Its pragmatic nature has made for something of a fragmented vision; however, it directly focuses on the need to balance out profitability with environmental profession.

MORALITY AND GREENING

This leads us back to the issue that was first raised in Chapter 1: if an action is visibly good for securing profits and for the firm, is it devoid of moral worth? The classical deontological vision would hold that this is indeed the case; actions are only ethical if they are for the 'right' motives. Indeed, it could be argued that the process of greening is part-and-parcel of the amoralization of social life; invariably firms sell environmental awareness purely on the basis of profit (Crane 2000). Thus, the environment is reduced to little more than one of 'issue selling' and 'image management'. From a postmodern perspective, Zygmunt Bauman has depicted managers as locked into a 'self-sustaining rationality' within the firm, with their moral responsibility ceasing once the customer's requirements are met (Crane 2000; see also Bauman 1993).

There is an emerging school of thought that business has an ethical responsibility to become more proactive in dealing with environmental issues than simply the bottom line (Hoffman 1997: 232). Indeed, Hoffman (1997: 233) argues that business requires vision, commitment and courage, risk and sacrifice in providing much needed moral leadership, transcending the view that protecting the environment is desirable because, in many areas, it is demonstrably good for business. Welford (1995: 26) argues that truly sustainable development demands a global approach, a reconsideration of equity and a new stress on equality, and is based on firm moral foundations.

ENVIRONMENTAL MANAGEMENT SYSTEMS

There has been increasing interest in Environmental Management Systems (EMS). An EMS:

- serves as a tool to improve environmental performance
- provides a systematic way of managing an organization's environmental affairs
- is the aspect of the organization's overall management structure that addresses immediate and long-term impacts of its products, services and processes on the environment
- gives order and consistency for organizations to address environmental concerns through the allocation of resources, assignment of responsibility and ongoing evaluation of practices, procedures and processes
- focuses on continual improvement of the system.

It can be argued that EMSs can be deployed by a wide range of profit and not-for-profit organizations. The key elements of an EMS include the following:

- *Policy statement* – a statement of the organization's commitment to the environment.
- *Identification of significant environmental impacts* – environmental attributes of products, activities and services and their effects on the environment.
- *Development of objectives and targets* – environmental goals for the organization.
- *Implementation* – plans to meet objectives and targets.
- *Training* – ensure that employees are aware and capable of their environmental responsibilities.
- *Management review.*

There is little doubt that the rise of EMS reflects the increasing concern of governments and firms with environmental issues. Critics of EMS argue that the approach is unnecessarily mechanistic, and the formulation of elaborate statements of intent can serve as little more than a smokescreen for a lack of concrete action.

ENVIRONMENTAL ISSUES AND THE LAW

In almost all developed nations, there is a plethora of legislation governing environmental issues. For example, in the United States, this has resulted in an Environmental Protection Agency, which regulates air and water quality on behalf of the general public. However, national standards differ greatly between nations – typically Western European standards are more stringent than US ones (Currie and Skolnik 1988: 305). In the third world, environmental standards and monitoring tend to be lax. This may have the effect of encouraging firms to aggressively 'regime shop' – in this case, relocating 'messy' activities to countries where controls are weak. Moreover, in some areas – most notably waste water treatment in the case of the UK – it may pay firms to pay nominal fines rather than clean up their acts. However, here the situation is rapidly changing. Envirowise, a UK government-backed environmental body, has warned firms that they face increasingly hefty fines if they do not comply with eco-legislation (*Financial Times* 30/6/2001). Ecowise research has revealed that 75 per cent of small firms in the UK are unclear as to how environmental regulations affect their operations (*Financial Times* 30/6/2001). This has led to the establishment of the Environmental Business Network, which keeps firms up to date with changes in the law.

SUMMARY

It is often assumed that poverty is a major cause of environmental degradation, when, of course, the bulk of damage to the world's environment is caused by the advanced societies (Brennan 1993). Industrial growth and a rise in net incomes are not going to solve the great environmental questions facing today's world. There is little doubt that it cannot be business as usual; indeed, growing numbers of firms are stressing the importance of green issues. However, this is rarely couched in moral terms; a more common argument is that taking care of the environment makes increasing commercial sense. In many cases, this is undoubtedly correct, however, it can be argued that there is a need for business to take environmental issues more seriously as an ethical concern. The deontological view that apparently ethical actions when prompted solely by commercial criteria are devoid of moral worth can be contested – the utilitarian response would be that it is surely better to have good actions than bad, no matter what the underlying motivation. Nonetheless, there is a case for the argument that the sheer scale of environmental degradation, which has threatened the entire biosphere, requires a more radical change in attitudes amongst commercial firms towards the environment; it can no longer be 'business as usual'.

KEY QUESTIONS
....

1. Why should firms take environmental issues seriously? Give reasons for your answer.
2. Introduce and critically discuss the 'hard green' perspective.
3. Introduce and critically discuss the 'deep ecology' perspective.
4. Should there be more to corporate environmental responsibility than the desire to secure long-term profits? Give reasons for your answer.

CASE STUDY: THE CONSEQUENCES OF 'SCORCHED EARTH' PRACTICE
....

'Asian Pulp and Paper (APP) is caught in a vicious circle. Because it has used relatively cheap timber culled from the rainforests, it has been able to undercut competitors and so depress the global paper market.

But now it finds itself with huge debts, in part caused by this depressed market. It is having to service the deficit by driving up production – and cutting down more trees. When all the Indonesian forests are gone, there could be a world paper shortage and spiralling prices.

APP has international debts of £8.5 billion, and its share price plummeted from £5 to 8p before dealing was suspended. Normally bankruptcy would quickly follow this situation, but a financial conjuring trick by the Indonesian government has kept APP afloat.

The government took over the local bank to which APP owed most money, making it the preferential creditor. Investors would get little or nothing if they forced the company into bankruptcy.

As a result APP can go on cutting forests until it runs out of trees. According to *Science* magazine: "If the current state of resource anarchy continues, the lowland forests of the Sundra shelf, the richest forests on earth, will be destroyed by 2005 in Sumatra".

Prominent in the destruction is the APP subsidiary Indah Kiat, the vast paper and pulp plant which is accused of getting large quantities of cheap timber supplies by clear cutting tropical rainforest.

One Indah Kiat supervisor told the *Guardian*: "There's no hurry to use more sustainable wood because that's more expensive to process. So we are using tropical hardwood and not asking too many questions about how legal it is".

British investors are among those who have ploughed money into APP. NatWest led a syndicate to provide £50 million for companies within the APP group, and its current lending remains at £7 million. A Friends of the Earth report, *Paper Tiger: Hidden Dragons*, claims that Barclays arranged a £430 million loan in September 1990. The bank has refused to comment. Legal and General has holdings worth £120,000 in Indah Kiat and another subsidiary, Tjiwi Kimia, but is to review them. London-based Newton Investment Management is reported to be the 19th biggest shareholder in APP, with stock worth £1.4 million – it refused to comment.

Ed Matthew, Friends of the Earth forests campaigner, said APP's trouble "would never have reached this stage if international investors had not put money into the company so it could go on building bigger plants. This led to them clear cutting even more rainforest, so flooding the market with cheap paper. Because the paper is so cheap the company has not been able to pay its debts, creating a vicious circle of more destruction and more debt".' (*Guardian* 26/7/2001).

ISSUES

The above case raises a range of key questions. First, how accountable should financial institutions be for the actions of their customers: should banks loan money when it is evident that such money may be used to support palpably unethical activities? Secondly, would a more hardline approach by the banks at this stage – if prompted solely by the parlous financial state of APP – be devoid of moral worth?

FURTHER READING

Attfield, R. 1999. *The Ethics of the Global Environment*. Edinburgh: Edinburgh University Press. A useful general account, encompassing a range of pressing issues and debates in environmental ethics.

Berry, R.J. (ed.). 1993. *Environmental Dilemmas: Ethics and Decisions*. London: Chapman and Hall. Again, a useful general and applied introduction to environmental debates.

Crane, A. 2000. 'Corporate greening as amoralization', *Organizational Studies*, 21, 4: 673–96. An interesting critique of the conventional wisdom surrounding environmental issues.

Singer, P. 1995. *Practical Ethics*. Cambridge: Cambridge University Press. Singer deals with a range of environmental issues in this work. Indeed, this book constitutes a major contribution to debates on environmental ethics.

ETHICS IN A GLOBALIZING WORLD

Increasingly, firms are under pressure to compete in a global marketplace, given a general tendency to deregulation, reduced state involvement, and the increased mobility of investor capital. On the one hand, whilst holding undoubted risks, this process opens up new markets and opportunities for firms based in the advanced societies. On the other hand, with these opportunities comes a range of responsibilities and obligations: firms have the same duty to be ethical in both mature and emerging markets. However, more contentious is the extent and range of ethical concerns that should be universal, and what forms of behaviour are acceptable in different national contexts, particularly given the exigencies of competition and pressures for development.

COMPREHENDING GLOBALIZATION

The concept of 'globalization' is an extremely loose one: there has been considerable debate as to its nature and implications (beyond the scope of this chapter). However, it is commonly assumed to result in a greater convergence in terms of state policies and workplace practices (Szaban and Henderson 1998: 586). A central debate revolves around the extent to which national social formations can still be regarded as sites of institutions capable of determining political and economic outcomes for a population in question (Szaban and Henderson 1998: 586).

Keohone and Nye define globalization as a 'state of the world involving networks of interdependence at multi-continental distance' (quoted in Morrissey and Filatotchev 2000). Late twentieth-century globalization is particularly characterized by considerable diversity and interdependence in such networks. Globalization is not new: global trade has been around for thousands of years (McIntosh 2000). However, what has changed is the size and scope of business organizations, the dramatic increase in private investment, and the ability to access information and communicate 24 hours a day (McIntosh 2000).

There is little doubt that the process of globalization is a contentious one (cf. Sklair 1996): its benefits have, to date, been highly uneven. The economic performance of tropical Africa, and large areas of Eastern Europe, has, for example, lagged far behind the advanced societies in the 1990s (Morrissey and Filatotchev 2000). At least 400 million people continue to lack the calories, protein, vitamins and minerals to sustain their bodies and minds in a healthy state (Singer 1995: 218). The Worldwatch Institute estimates that about 1.2 billion people – 23 per cent of the earth's population – live in absolute poverty: 'a condition of life so characterized by malnutrition, illiteracy, disease, squalid surroundings, high infant mortality and low life expectancy as to be beneath any reasonable definition of human decency' (Singer 1995: 219). Indeed, the material conditions of many demonstrably worsened in the 1990s.

These developmental problems have variously been ascribed to a lack of investment in human resource development and infrastructure, the role of global buyers and distribution networks, the fundamental inability of many third world firms that previously enjoyed the backing of overly protectionist states, and/or incomplete deregulation. However, it should be noted that even in the advanced societies, many industries base their continued prosperity on protectionism or state intervention in some form or another (this could range from anti-dumping measures to lavish defence contracts awarded to local firms). In addition, it can be argued that bodies such as the World Trade Organization (WTO) may exacerbate existing inequalities under certain circumstances: there is a need to 'consider the distribution side of globalization' (Morrissey and Filatotchev 2000). The uneven – and unequal – process of globalization underscores the importance of central questions such as the universality of core ethical issues, and whether basic mores of behaviour can transcend legal and political boundaries (Payne *et al.* 1997).

As McIntosh (2000) notes, questions such as global poverty are generally not seen as a major issue on the agenda of global business. However, it can be argued that, if business wants to promote a global economy and free trade, it has to be able to argue that the benefits will be felt by all the world's people, 'not just the few': 'poverty is not the business of business, but business should be part of the solution to resolve poverty, not part of the problem' (McIntosh 2000).

THE RISE AND IMPACT OF TRANSNATIONAL CORPORATIONS (TNCs)

As Jackson (1997) notes, TNCs have to contend with a 'layered array' of local, national and international rules and norms. TNCs control 80 per cent of the world's land cultivated for export orientated crops, whilst many TNCs have a turnover larger than the gross national product of entire nations and regions (Dobson 1992). Western corporate culture has itself become increasingly transnational (Dobson 1992). TNCs have often been depicted as agents of global uniformity, of economic and cultural hegemony, underscoring the importance of ethical issues in this regard.

Globalization has led to a greater awareness of the problems of corporate governance, and increasing pressures for reforms: even entire models of operation (for example, of the Chaebols in Korea) have been questioned. The financial community has become increasingly aware of the need for greater self-regulation. (Vinten 2000: 173).

However, 'much of the need to encourage firm corporate governance...hangs on the supply of suitable director, shareholder, and perchance, stakeholder information' (Vinten 2000: 177). The Barings Bank affair – resulting in the bankruptcy of a major financial institution as a result of the activities of a single 'rogue trader' – did not involve the violation of abstract ethical principles, but outright forgery and fraud (Jackson 1997). It also revealed the intense difficulty firms may experience when they try and supervise remote operations, especially those where key decisions are delegated to a relatively small number of staff members in a remote locale. Moreover, it became evident that there was no systematic and comprehensive way of gauging corporate liability at transnational level (Jackson 1998).

Even within countries, there is often considerable variation in laws and enforcement between provinces, states or regions (Payne *et al.* 1997). Such variations are considerably greater at the international level: TNCs have to analyse, assess and amalgamate heterogeneous legal regimes (Payne *et al.* 1997). They also face the problems of transferring domestic ethical norms into an international context, attempts that are often stillborn in the face of competing pressures ranging from profitability to cultural variations.

Moreover, there is little doubt that many TNCs engage in regime shopping, locating contentious activities in countries where there are fewer legal restrictions, or where law enforcement is perceived to be weak or erratic.

For example, in 1998, following on protracted deliberations, the Irish Supreme Court found that US chemical manufacturer, Merk, had deliberately and wilfully discharged noxious chemicals in the hope that this would go unnoticed in surrounding communities (Dobson 1992).

Oil companies operating in the Amazon basin routinely construct roads – even when transport alternatives such as water exist – opening up remote areas of tropical rain forest to clear cut logging and slash and burn agriculture (Dobson 1992). Third world governments are often reluctant to challenge activities of TNCs given the omnipresent threat of the latter relocating to countries where legal restrictions may be even weaker. In short, market pressures may undermine the scope of deregulation (Diller 1999).

A firm may operate in a number of different countries, and may be faced with a range of ethical quandaries, even if it keeps scrupulously to the law in host nations. Indeed, Maynard (2001) argues that TNCs find themselves 'on the margins of morality', given the great diversity in historical, cultural and government mores in different nations.

In a large part of the world, basic human rights are still little more than a dream (Donaldson 1991: 139). How TNCs should operate in such environments has been the subject of considerable debate: should authoritarian regimes be isolated and starved of investment capital, or should every effort be made to draw them into the global system, which will make it harder to retain anachronistic political institutions?

Moreover, even in democratic poor countries with reasonably good governance, a wide range of ethical dilemmas exist. This would include the growing of export crops in areas where widespread starvation exists (Donaldson 1991: 139). Poor countries consume 180 kilos of grain a year per person, compared to 900 in the United States. The difference being in the West is that most of the grain produced is fed to animals, to support a diet that contains far more animal products than what those in the South eat. Indeed, as Singer (1995: 220) notes, 'if we stopped feeding animals on grains and soybeans, the amount of food saved would – if distributed amongst those who need it – be more than enough to end hunger throughout the world' (Singer 1995: 220). Whilst many would shy away from so radical a solution, it is evident that even the cultivation of food crops in the developing world – and what is done with the produce – poses definite ethical dilemmas.

The above-mentioned issue of toxic waste is another issue: because of safety measures in the West, some of the world's poorest nations end up as dumping grounds for waste (Donaldson 1991). This is achieved by means of legal loopholes, bribery, or simply large fees in countries where legislation is incomplete. It can be argued that even if a third world government accepts responsibility for taking waste, it can still be extremely problematic: there are often inadequate safeguards to ensure that any benefits will reach the affected communities, or that adequate safeguards are adhered to (Donaldson 1991).

In the end, TNCs have four moral agencies providing some boundaries as to what is acceptable conduct: internal in terms of managerial ideologies and corporate codes of ethics; other competitors; governmental agencies; and public pressure especially given the activities 'of NGOs and offshore watchdog bodies'. However, competitors may often be reluctant to draw attention to unethical behaviour, as it may represent a useful way of internal cost cutting in the future (Donaldson 1991). In other words, firms may be reluctant to blow the whistle on unethical actions by others; in order to keep their own strategic options open. Meanwhile, host governments may be reluctant to question actions by investors if they face the threat that firms will simply relocate if faced with greater regulatory pressure. Already, there has been a slow drift of firms from Thailand to China, on account of the greater number of regulations (still very modest) in the former.

However, parent governments (i.e. of states where TNCs have their head office) may have considerably greater clout. There is little doubt that the US Foreign Corrupt Practices Act – which, seeks to combat bribery of foreign officials – has had considerable influence. This has been both in terms of restricting what US firms may do, and in terms of US government pressure on other governments, in order to 'level the playing field' and ensure that US firms do not compete at a disadvantage with foreign ones (Zagaris and Ohri 1999). Indeed, a number of other Western governments have enacted measures to combat international corruption.

However, the practice of bribery is deeply embedded within certain national contexts; it is extremely difficult to design institutional mechanisms to combat something that may have been widely accepted as part and parcel with doing business for centuries (Zagaris and Ohri 1999). In addition, they are many grey areas, surrounding the payment of 'facilitation fees', semi-official taxes and the like, making enforcement of anti-bribery measures difficult. More invidious is a frequent lack of will. Firms can engage in a range of practices to conceal the payment of bribes, especially if they fear that a failure to make illegal payments may result in a vital loss of business (Zagaris and Ohri 1999). Nonetheless, Maynard (2001) argues that the threat of public exposure probably represents the greatest check on unethical actions by TNCs.

More contentious are suggestions that the practice of 'dumping' – where a foreign firm offers goods in a particular market at considerably less than the price for the same goods elsewhere, and sometimes at below cost – constitutes an unethical act. Several governments – most notably that of the United States – have enacted anti-dumping measures. However, as Delener (1998) notes, the business practice of offering discounts is not generally seen as immoral. Indeed, predatory pricing by domestic firms to drive out competitors (local or foreign) is commonly seen as acceptable – an ethical problem only arises if the goods may constitute a health hazard, such as cigarettes. Indeed, it can be argued that 'dumping' has few ethical implications, but simply represents a response to a situation where global over-production exists (Delener 1998).

Proponents of the role of TNCs have tended to fall into two categories. First, there are the followers of the neo-liberal school, or modified versions thereof. An example of the latter, Dobson (1992) suggests that rather than attempting to decide what constitutes ethical behaviour, managers – who are simply agents – should leave the matter to their principles, who are best equipped to make ethical choices that are also economically optimal. In short, managers of TNCs face few ethical dilemmas, and should simply carry out the instructions of their principles, whilst seeking to maximize profitability. However, Dobson (1992) tempers his argument by suggesting that principles do not simply constitute shareholders (as is suggested by writers such as Friedman), but rather all relevant stakeholders.

Secondly, there are modernization theorists (in the broad tradition of writers such as Rostow), who argue that, given their undoubted economic muscle, as well as their role in shaping global culture, TNCs have the potential to bring about a considerably better world. For example, Buller *et al.* (quoted in Rallapalli 1999) suggest that instead of being part of a problem, TNCs have the capacity to be part of a solution in promoting more ethical conduct on account of their global influence. In short, they represent part and parcel of the modernization process, and their activities will invariably contribute to modernization in both domestic and social life.

GLOBAL CODES OF ETHICS

It can be argued that attempts to deal with transnational ethical issues by unilateral or bilateral government actions leads to an unjust situation for both victim and perpetrator: enforcement is very difficult, and regulatory institutions will be incomplete (Jackson 1998). Moreover, firms bound by the restrictive laws of a parent nation will be at an automatic disadvantage vis-à-vis those falling under weaker regulatory regimes (ibid.): ethical behaviour in a globalizing world requires global ethical commitments. Jackson (1998) argues that, given that TNCs have reaped the benefits of the globalization of markets, they should assume some of the responsibilities that comes with this, by binding themselves to internationally relevant codes of ethics.

A range of international organizations – most notably trading blocs such as the European Union (EU) and the North American Free Trade Area (NAFTA), the International Labour Organization, the OECD, and the United Nations – have all attempted to promote minimum ethical standards amongst firms operating in their member nations. However, such codes have tended to be very vague, in order to avoid disputes as to what constitutes acceptable behaviour in different cultural contexts (cf. Payne *et al.* 1997).

On the one hand, corporate social responsibility has become a global trend, not just the purview of the north (Leipziger 2000: 39). For example, throughout Latin America, there has been great interest in corporate codes of conduct on labour standards. On the other hand, Latin American firms (and, indeed, their Asian counterparts) are generally still less committed to independent monitoring than their northern counterparts (Leipziger 2000: 39). In part this reflects the persistence of corruption as a prerequisite for doing business in many regions, despite the general rise of an independent press and a stronger civil society (Leipziger 2000: 40).

In addition, there are a number of international conventions to restrict corrupt practices, examples being the 1996 Inter-American Convention on Corruption, and the 1997 OECD Anti-Bribery Convention ('The Convention on Combating Bribery of Foreign Government Officials in International Business Transactions'). However, implementation and enforcement of these conventions remain extremely difficult. For example, whilst the Inter-American Convention requires signatories to prohibit domestic and foreign bribes and to actively combat the illegal enrichment of government officials, it lacks substantial mechanisms for monitoring and enforcement (Zagaris and Ohri 1999). Meanwhile, the OECD Convention obliges signatories to criminalize the bribery of officials, and provides the basis for international judicial cooperation. However, the governments that are party to the agreement continue to deal with corrupt practices in an uneven and not always transparent fashion (see Zagaris and Ohri 1999).

In a review of international accords, which include ethical guidelines for TNCs, reached over the years 1948–88, Frederick (1991) found that the bulk of guidelines aim to shape practices with regard to employment relations, consumer protection, the environment, political participation and basic human rights. However, their moral authority was based on the competing principles of national sovereignty, social equity, market integrity and universal human rights. Deontological principles would suggest the primacy of questions of human rights, although utilitarians could argue that long-term environmental issues are of equal or greater importance. In practice, codes have tended to focus on the former, however (Rallappalli 1999).

There is little doubt that growing numbers of TNCs do pay lip service to such codes, although ensuring their operational acceptance is somewhat more difficult (Rallappalli 1999). In addition, many TNCs have their own, internal, codes. However, there is considerable variability in such codes, although most are founded on rights-based principles, including an agreement to treat all employees fairly with regard to wages, working conditions and benefits (Maynard 2001). Moreover, there is a general absence of protection for whistle blowers, whilst questionable behaviour can often be passed off as simply a product of cultural differences (Maynard 2001).

Indeed, international codes of ethics remain dogged by inconsistency in scope and coverage, and the characteristic 'looseness' of implementation and assessment (Diller 1999). Moreover, if they are to escape being protectionist, ethical codes have to actively seek to promote capacity development within the third world, to actively offer support via concrete and targeted programmes (Diller 1999). Payne *et al.* (1997) argue that an effective internal ethical code should incorporate not just moral, but also cultural and managerial concerns, and should go beyond being simply a public relations gambit aimed at proving 'one can shop without guilt'. They suggest that firms have specific duties, which encompass basic human rights issues, environmental protection, fair employment practices and consumer protection (Payne *et al.* 1997). However, Getz (quoted in Payne *et al.* 1997) asserts that firms have a more comprehensive range of obligations. This would include the need to promote local participation (and the use of local suppliers and local equity participation), reinvestment, refraining from corrupt practices and unlawful or improper political activity, keeping to the law and engaging in technology transfers. Of course, the value of some of these enjoinders in contexts where the government is overly repressive – such as the former apartheid government in South Africa – can be contested. Perhaps in such contexts, firms have a moral obligation to defy civil authority under certain circumstances.

Drawing on the rights-based view that underlies most international codes of ethics, Donaldson (1991) argues that there are a number of international rights that are grounded fundamentally. Such rights protect things of extreme importance and are subject to recurring threats, whilst the obligations imposed are fair and economically affordable given the distribution of burdens generally (what Nickel calls affordability-fairness) (Donaldson 1991). These could include the following international rights (Donaldson 1991):

- The right to freedom of physical movement.

- The right to ownership of property.
- The right to freedom from torture; the right to a fair trial.
- The right to non-discriminatory treatment (for example, on grounds of race or gender).
- The right to physical security.
- The right to freedom of speech and association.
- The right to minimal education.
- The right to political participation.
- The right to subsistence.

Other rights could include that to a basic standard of living, as might be prescribed by Rawls' difference principle (Donaldson 1991). TNCs can honour some of these rights simply by avoidance (ibid.). Nonetheless, there is little doubt that TNCs do have some obligations that go beyond abstaining from depriving directly. For example, no firm can wholly neglect issues such as hunger, racism or political oppression (Vinten 2000). However, many practices may be a subject of great controversy. For example, the aggressive promotion of high yield seeds and fertilizers may increase food output, but may also lock peasants in a cycle of debt.

CULTURAL RELATIVISM AND UNIVERSALS

The increasing role of transnational corporations makes some cross-cultural conflict inevitable (Buller *et al.* 1997). Indeed, different social and cultural factors will result in very different ethical concerns. To Hofstede (1980), culture provides the basis for distinction between different groups and is reflected in the values and beliefs of a particular society: culture shapes what people see in a situation, and delineates appropriate behaviour. Hofstede (1980) argues that culture is a form of 'collective mental programming', and incorporates four dimensions, including the individualism/collectivism nexus, masculinity/feminism, power distance, and uncertainty avoidance. One's cultural make-up will, in turn, determine one's approach to a range of ethical dilemmas.

International ethics involves an attempt to apply a specific set of moral values in situations involving two or more nations (Buller *et al.* 1997). However, it can be argued that universal moral norms tend to be general and rather abstract; what constitutes 'fairness', for example, can be open to very different interpretations in different sets of cultural circumstances.

For example, vigorously implementing an equal opportunities policy may result in cultural condemnation, loss of customer and client contacts, and eventual unprofitability of the entire firm (Mayer and Cava 1993). On other hand, it is hard to maintain cultural particularism in globalizing world, and the negative impact of 'doing things differently' should not be underestimated, nor the positive benefits from pursuing equity (Mayer and Cava 1993).

Numerous different writers have suggested ways out of this quandary. Donaldson (1991), for example, from a rights-based perspective, suggests that if an ethical contestation is based on economic concerns, TNCs should consider whether a particular practice would be permissible in the home country, if it were at the same stage of development as the host country. However, it could be argued that child labour, for example – which was tolerated in most Western countries a century or so ago – is unacceptable, whatever the economic circumstances.

Mayer and Cava (1993) argue that, without 'slavishly adhering' to Western equity legislation, the aim should be to promote equity in a low key way: there is a need for some basic minimum principles and morals, without the 'ethical balkanization' that full on relativism would entail. Values should be universally discovered to be shared, whilst universal standards should come out of experience, an example being the increasing global commitment to at least the form of multi-part democracy.

Donaldson goes on to suggest that if the causes of an ethical dispute are not economic, then a practice is only permissible if it is necessary to do business in the host country and does not violate fundamental international rights. Again, this could be contested. For example, De George (1986) suggests that each situation requires judgement and moral imagination (which would, of course, reflect the utilitarian approach). However, he further suggests that there is a need for practices, procedures and background institutions to reinforce ethical behaviour – people and firms need encouragement to make sound ethical judgements.

Jackson (1997) argues that, whilst cultural specificities must be acknowledged, there is a core of ethical values common to all societies. It is possible to encode this, but, in the end, the internal 'atmosphere' of the organization will largely shape behaviour. Such an ethical core, would, for example, encompass a rejection of overt racial discrimination (Jackson 1997). However, even in this area, there is considerable room for contention. This would include the extent and scope of affirmative action programmes, and the degree to which other forms of discrimination may be unacceptable. For example, in many conservative societies in the developing world, a far higher degree of gender discrimination is enforced than would be acceptable in the developed world. Less morally contentious issues would include a rejection of slavery, theft, outright deception, fraud and the like. Jackson (1997) asserts that, given that many ethical concerns are shared, ethical codes can rise above national parochialisms. Indeed, conduct can be guided by the Kantian enjoinder never to simply treat people as a means, without taking account of their personal needs and rights.

THINKING ABOUT GLOBAL TRADE AND RELATIONS – RECENT PERSPECTIVES

As Moody (1997: 6) notes, despite globalization, 'the world remains a very uneven, fragmented and divided one'; indeed, 'the process of deepening international economic integration actually increases some aspects of fragmentation and inequality between nations'. World systems theory holds that global capitalism must, of necessity, continually increase production and trade, to guarantee the political conditions for this to take place world-wide, and to constantly restimulate consumer demand (Sklair 1995: 62). This in turn led to the emergence of the 'more precise and research rich' concept of Global Commodity Chains (GCCs), first propounded by Gereffi and Korzeniewicz (Sklair 1995: 40). Producers, intermediaries and buyers are seen as forming part of the same global organization, in ever-increasing networks of GCCs (Sklair 1995: 62). Of course, what matters is who is most powerful in the chain (Morrissey and Filatotchev 2000).

GCC theory holds that TNCs, or, failing that, end-users, represent the most powerful links in the chain (Szaban and Henderson 1998: 587). Although many of the underlying assumptions of GCC theory may be contested, there is little doubt that global inequality greatly increased within the 1980s and 1990s (Moody 1997). Patterns of trade are likely to strengthen the strong and more powerful, at the expense of weaker nations or regions. This has led to periodic calls for a review of existing relationships, and for 'fairer trade', calls which have become increasingly part of the mainstream discourse, and that growing numbers of TNCs have been forced to pay at least lip service to. However, there remains considerable debate as to solutions. Neo-liberals would suggest that this reflects market imperfection, and a failure to fully deregulate. Meanwhile, their critics would argue that a greater range of institutional mechanisms need to be erected to 'balance out' the flows of trade, in terms of national legislation, transnational conventions and accords, and via greatly strengthened international codes of ethics.

A broader question is whether the richer regions of the world have some or other duty to help the poor. This is an obligation that is distinct from questions of ownership and property: one can believe in property rights and the desirability of the market system, yet retain a sense of duty towards the poor (Singer 1995: 234). The question emerges as to whether aid to the poorer parts of the world should be left to governments, rather than troubling firms or the conscience of the individual. As noted in earlier chapters, writers such as Friedman have suggested that the main obligation of the firm is towards those that own it: it is undesirable that management engage in philanthropic activity, in effect spending the money of others.

However, only a handful of countries give more than 0.7 per cent of their GDP in aid to the world's poorer regions. Indeed, the United States gives only one-sixth of 1 per cent (Singer 1995: 241). Singer (1995: 241) suggests that there is no reason to believe governments will give more if individual contributions decreased, and an ethical obligation rests on all to improve the overall human (and, indeed, global) condition.

SUMMARY

Globalization is a widely deployed and little understood concept. However, it can be simply understood as the process by which national social formations – and the autonomy of national governments – have become eroded as a result of the unification of markets and of consumer taste, and the increasing global mobility of financial capital. The globalization of corporate activities is not a new process, but rather one that has been underway for over a century. However, there is little doubt that this process has been greatly accelerated, and opens up a range of ethical dilemmas for firms operating across national boundaries. These include the identification of ethical principles that are universal and should be consistently upheld (as adverse to culturally specific morals guidelines), approaches to trade and competition, and, indeed, even the extent to which firms should be more proactive in alleviating global poverty. Whilst, despite the proliferation of global ethical codes, clear solutions remain elusive, it is evident that firms are increasingly under pressure – from governments, NGOs, international organizations, and the public at large – to take global ethical issues seriously.

KEY QUESTIONS

1. What do you understand by the concept of globalization? Does this process pose any specific ethical dilemmas for firms?
2. Introduce the principal ethical challenges most likely to confront a transnational corporation.
3. What do you understand by the concept of 'fair trade'? Should this affect how firms do business in the developing world?

CASE STUDY: OIL CONCESSIONS IN ANGOLA: PUSHING THE LIMITS OF ETHICAL BEHAVIOUR?

The West African state of Angola has been wracked by a bloody civil war for over 25 years. Most of the Angolan oil industry is located in shallow water reserves offshore, safely removed from the activities of the rebel UNITA movement. However, advances in oil extraction technology have opened the way for the exploitation of vast deep water (1500 to 5000 feet below sea level) and ultra-deep water reserves (5000 and 7000 feet). Current oil production is 750 000 barrels a day, although this is likely to rise substantially in the future.

Angola's offshore oil is particularly attractive owing to a desire by international firms to diversify supplies away from the Middle East and geological factors. Angolan seismic data makes it relatively easy for firms to accurately target their drilling, with a success rate of 60–70 per cent as adverse to a world average of only 10 per cent.

The oil industry is jointly run by foreign firms, and the state oil firm, Sonangol. There has been intensive competition between Western petrochemicals companies for exploitation rights on recently identified ultra-deep water blocks. There is little doubt that US firms are at a substantial disadvantage vis-à-vis a number of European firms on account of more rigorous anti-bribery legislation.

The bulk of oil revenue is diverted through secret defence accounts, ostensibly in the interests of national security, although this has created considerable opportunities for the expropriation of oil revenue by a notoriously voracious state elite. Given the diversion of oil revenues into the personal accounts of senior government officials, on the military and to service foreign debt, only some 7 per cent of the annual budget was devoted to public expenditure by 1998.

The aggressive jockeying among Western petrochemicals firms for Angolan concessions, and controversies surrounding the payment of signature bonuses led to renewed questions being asked about the role of other petrochemicals firms in Angola in the aftermath of the Angolagate scandal. The latter implicated several senior government officials and oil firms in a complex illegal arms, oil and debt deal.

In Angola, a number of petrochemicals companies – including TotalElfFina, BP and Chevron – have been making substantial donations to the official Social Bonus Fund. The secretive manner in which these donations is being spent has led the newsletter, *Africa Confidential*, to charge that the social spending of oil companies in Angola could become 'another vehicle for (extending) credit to the Angolan elite' (*Africa Confidential* 15/9/2000).

ISSUES

Do you think that oil firms should invest in Angola at all, and what is ethically acceptable in the current scramble for ultra-deep water concessions? Should companies enquire too closely into the business of charitable concerns that are favoured by, or have close links to undoubtedly corrupt governments that are in the position to grant lucrative concessions? Thirdly, there is the perennial 'free rider' problem: there is little doubt that any oil firm that withdraws from Angola will soon be replaced by other, less principled, entrants. Should this, in any way, affect the decisions oil companies must make in dealing with the Angolan state elite?

FURTHER READING

Diller, J. 1999. 'A social conscience of the global marketplace', *International Labour Review*, 138, 2: 99–129. A useful coverage of ethical issues emerging from the global integration of markets.

Dobson, J. 1992. 'Ethics in the transnational corporation: the "moral buck" street', *Journal of Business Ethics*, 11, 1: 21–43. A provocative look at ethical issues concerning transnational corporations.

Freeman, R. (ed.). 1991. *Business Ethics: The State of the Art*. Oxford: Oxford University Press. This edited book accords considerable attention to the ethical dilemmas that emerge when firms operate across national boundaries.

PART II

ETHICAL MANAGEMENT IN PRACTICE

ETHICS AND HUMAN RESOURCE MANAGEMENT

During the last two decades the terrain of people management has seen heated debates and battles between the 'welfarists' – arguing that the primary job of human resources (HR) managers is to take care of the welfare of employees in the workplace – and 'managerialists'. The latter places considerably more emphasis on the *management* of people and considers HR as strategic factor, among others, in the competitive advantage equation. In this chapter we examine the recent rise of ethical concerns in contemporary human resource management (HRM) policies and practices in Western organizations. We discuss what constitute ethical HR practices and look at ethical rights, duties and obligations that organizations and employees have towards each other.

The classical conception of the relationship between employers and employees was based on the notion of a free contract between the two parties, essentially for their mutual benefit (Hoffman and Moore 1990: 269). Employers were expected to pay fair wages, and, in return, employees were to give their loyalty and obedience and above all satisfactory performance (Hoffman and Moore 1990). In modern organizations, however, the management of people is more complex and involves several stakeholders: the government, unions, shareholders, employees and management to mention a few (see Chapter 2). HRM management practices are strongly affected by the economic, political, technological, legal and social contexts within which they operate. These contexts pull the HRM function in different directions. Some HRM practices are more ethical than others – there is little doubt that some strategies for people management are patently unethical. While some writers argue for more protection to employees' interests and rights, others call for the protection of shareholders' interest at the expense of employees' rights and fair treatment.

IS HRM ETHICAL?

In an attempt to answer the question, Karen Legge noted that, 'Thirty years ago, the answer to the question "Is HRM ethical?" – certainly in the mind of the lay person – would probably have been: "Of course personnel management is ethical. It's there to help people, isn't it?" Personnel professionals, at least publicly, might have gone a long with this and pointed to the supposed origins of people management in benevolent paternalism and social welfare. But if asked the same question today, would there be a more hesitant response? First there would be some difficulty in presenting "one consistent image"' (1996: 34).

Several writers have covered the reasons for the rise of ethical concerns over contemporary HRM practices in considerable depth (Legge, 1996, 1998, 2000; Winstanley *et al.* 1996). One compelling reason would be that current

HRM models, policies and practices partially reflect the 1980s' and 1990s' macro-economic and political environments, characterized by global and cut-throat competition. They focused management concerns on survival and achieving sustainable competitive advantage by obtaining higher than average returns on investment. Obviously, these exigencies would, in most cases, make managers unsympathetic to ethical HRM practices unless they are proven to help the company achieve its strategic advantage or at least do not damage it. In addition, in the UK, successive Conservative governments, and even New Labour, have given management a relatively free hand to improve the economy's competitiveness by doing what they see fit. Legge (1988: 150) noted that:

> There was no 'other alternative', if a cure (for the British disease) was to be effected, then a strong dose of monetarism and market competition was in order, never mind if the side effects....threatened to kill the patent. Such medicine was seen as the *right* way to combat the evils of low productivity, high inflation and poor competitiveness.

As a result, the HRM function during the last two decades has embodied managerialist values focusing its aim primarily on helping the organization achieve and sustain its competitive advantage at any cost. Keenoy (1990) describes the HRM function in the 1980s as a 'wolf in sheep's clothing'.

The new business environment created two types of HRM models sometimes practised simultaneously by the same firm. First, a 'hard' model of HRM characterized by strict control, high job insecurity, a model that saw employees as a cost to be minimized rather than an asset to be developed. Secondly, a more humane 'soft' model of HRM, seeing employees as assets that need to be developed and nurtured because they are relevant to the company's corporate strategy and viewed as a key source of competitive advantage.

Since the 1980s, several alternative models of HRM have been proposed. Beer *et al.* (1984) suggested a HRM model based on flexibility and commitment and argued that managing people humanly enhances performance. In the UK, David Guest (1987) proposed a similar model based on integration, commitment, flexibility and quality, and argued for similar causality. Several other models have been proposed since then – 'high performance work practices' (Huselid 1995), 'high commitment management' (Wood quoted in Legge 1998: 152), and the 'HR-based view' to mention a few. The HR-based view model links the management of people to the firm's core competency and looks for ways – 'best practices' – to achieve sustainable competitive advantage through the *management* of people. As a result of these developments, both the workplace landscape and work force structure have significantly changed in ways that have raised increasing ethical concerns, for example, jobs are becoming less and less secure, management is using recruitment and surveillance techniques that trespass workers' 'zone of privacy', employees' values and social norms are being manipulated to create new corporate cultures and/or change the old one.

STRATEGIC HRM AND ETHICS

Thus, during the intense competitive environment of the 1980s and early 1990s, moral and ethical scruples were placed on the backburner, as managers looked for ways to survive the onslaught by the Japanese and more flexible Western competitors. Ethical and moral practices were plausible only if managers were convinced that they would not undermine their competitiveness or contribute to the company's quest to achieve a sustainable competitive advantage. Strategic HRM scholars such as Tsui (1987) have argued for the thesis of 'strategic fit' between HRM policies and practices, and the overall corporate strategy. In a business environment characterized by relentless competition and a quest for achieving and sustaining competitive advantage, the strategic role of the HRM function, it was argued, was to help the organization achieve its strategic goals regardless of whether HRM policies and practices are ethical or not. The key measuring criterion was as follows: do all practices help the company achieve a better than average return on investment?

ETHICS, HRM AND CORE AND PERIPHERAL WORKERS

Numerical flexibility has become a commonly accepted and increasingly attractive practice in most Western organizations (Hakim 1990). This new employment system creates winners as well as losers by dividing employees into core – winners – and periphery – losers. The former usually consists of a small highly skilled, multi-talented, sought after and nurtured individuals. They are regarded as core competencies and are unique – by possessing unique knowledge that is valuable to the company's strategy, hard or expensive to find in the labour market, and not easily substitutable by technology. Conversely, the latter group – periphery – are temporary workers employed under short-term fixed contracts and often paid hourly or weekly (Legge 1988). They have minimal training and few opportunities for promotion. They are powerless and often have their contracts terminated (or at least not rolled over) for arbitrary reasons (or for no reason at all). Peripheral workers are usually workers with skills that are not valuable to the company, easily available in the labour market, and/or their effective use does not require a long socialization process within the company. Legge (1996) noted that 'while members of the former (core) group are co-opted as permanent staff on rewarding contracts, peripheral employees are becoming a contingent workforce on non-standard contracts'. This core–periphery employment paradigm has created a dichotomy of workplace experiences. Payne and Wayland (1999) argue that many HR managers accept this dichotomy as 'taken for granted' treatment of employees. They speculated that this could be a result of the emerging 'new' HR mindset focusing more on business competitiveness and survival rather than on fair and humanistic treatment of employees. According to Payne and Wayland (1999), once HR managers start viewing employees as a 'resource' or a strategic means to achieving and sustaining competitive advantage, their cognitive mindset legitimates the grouping of employees into first-class 'core workers' and second- and third-class ' periphery' depending on their 'worth'. The latter is measured by their potential contribution to the firm's overall strategy. Legge (2000: 38) argues that 'there does seem to be some evidence, if perhaps rather trenchantly drawn, that an ethical HRM is more likely to be offered to core knowledge workers' rather than periphery workers. This is because a professional work force will not tolerate arbitrary and unfair treatment by employers. Similarly Purcell (quoted in Legge 2000: 32) questions the universal applicability of the 'ethical' model of managing people. Purcell suggests that 'soft' HRM practices are only applicable in very specific sets of circumstances and likely to be focused on a relatively small number of workplaces, and within them, on core employees.

HRM AND ETHICAL DILEMMAS

Because of the nature of the HRM function, HR managers must frequently make and implement decisions with ethical implications. This explains why HR managers want to make the HR department the organizational locus of responsibility for ethical behaviour at work. During the process of making and executing HRM policies and practices, HR managers, however, are often torn between strong conflicting pressures associated with the field (Hosmer 1987). HR is partially about enhancing commitment and boosting control, training and manipulation, surveillance and upholding the right to privacy, making provision for 'whistle blowing' and policing disloyalty, empowerment and change, to mention a few. Other dilemmas involving favouritism in employment – old boys' network, inconsistencies in pay (Heery 2000), sex and race discrimination, and breaches of confidentiality – face HR managers on a regular basis. Downsizing and outsourcing often lead to problems in maintaining employee motivation and sense of wellbeing in the face of growing job insecurity. There is no easy way to deal with these dilemmas. Winstanley and Woodall (2000: 278) note that 'HRM managers must

Rhetoric	Reality
Customer first	Market forces supreme
Total quality management	Doing more with less
Lean production	Mean production
Flexibility	Management 'can do' what it wants
Core and periphery	Reducing the organization's commitment
Devolution/delayering	Reducing the number of middle managers
Downsizing/right-sizing	Redundancy
New working patterns	Part-time instead of full-time jobs
Empowerment	Making someone else take the risk and responsibility
Training and development	Manipulation
Employability	No employment security
Recognizing contribution	Undermining the trade union of the individual and collective bargaining
Teamworking	Reducing the individual's discretion

Source: Legge, 1998: 155.

Figure 6.1 Sission's model of rhetoric and reality in HRM

inevitably confront ethical dilemmas, and that some of these may be neither apparent nor easily resolved'. This explains the extensively debated widening cleavage between rhetoric and reality in HRM (see Figure 6.1). In such a contradictory context, today's HRM managers and professionals are increasingly advised not to see their attitudes as dichotomous choices, but somehow to embrace 'paradox' as the simultaneous expression of diverse attitudes. HR managers are urged to strike a balance between these competing, and sometimes contradictory, values based on their reflection, personal experience and professional ethical codes of conduct. In her analysis of the ethics of HRM policy and practices, Karen Legge (1998) argues that because people are used as a means to an end – achieving sustainable competitive advantage – HRM decision making is firmly grounded in utilitarianism. She added that even the 'soft' model of HRM, which genuinely seeks to treat people in a humane way and would pass 'muster in terms of the deontologists', applied to all employees, has several embedded contradictions. Indeed:

> The contradictions embedded in HRM are illustrative of the Kantian dilemma that second-order moral rules can clash and that resolutions can often only be achieved by back-door admission of utilitarianism (Legge 1998: 162).

A survey conducted by the SHRM/ERC in the United States showed that 47 per cent of the HRM professionals surveyed reported that they 'feel pressured by other employees or managers to compromise their organization's standards of ethical business conduct in order to achieve business objectives'. Figure 6.2 shows that 'aggressive financial business objectives' are the main 'moralizing' factors – half of HRM professionals surveyed felt pressure

Meeting overly aggressive financial business objectives	50%
Meeting schedule pressures	38%
Helping the organization survive	30%
Rationalizing that others do it	22%
Resisting competitive threats	18%
Saving jobs	16%
Advancing the career interests of my boss	15%
Feeling peer pressure	12%
Advancing my own career or financial interests	4%

Source: SHRM/ERC Ethics Survey Snapshot (www.shrm.org).

Figure 6.2   Pressures experienced by HRM management

to compromise their ethical business conduct. Note that the first five key factors are related to the survival and wellbeing of the organization and not individuals. Only 16 per cent felt pressure to save jobs. Interestingly, the survey showed that HRM professionals do not compromise their ethics for personal gain (4 per cent).

HRM ETHICAL CODES OF CONDUCT

Many firms give HR managers a key leadership role in establishing and maintaining their ethical code of conduct (Driscoll and Hoffman 1998). This is often carried out through seeking – and providing – sources of ethical information and advice (Perry *et al.* 1990), as well as developing and executing ethical programmes (Driscoll and Hoffman 1998). As a result, certain aspects of HRM practices have become more formalized through the establishment of both professional codes of ethics within the HRM field, and the internal codes of conduct within many Western corporations. To outsiders, codes of conduct are the most visible sign of a company's ethical policy. In the UK, the ranks of companies gaining the IIP (Investor in People) status has rapidly swelled; the certification process includes a commitment to ethical HRM practices (See IPD 1997). Similarly, in the USA, the certification process is often linked to espoused goals of creating an ethical organization culture (Payne and Wayland 1999: 300). Again, a survey of 1500 US employees showed that the percentage of employees reporting that their organization had in place a set of written ethical standards increased from 60 per cent in 1994 to 79 per cent in 1999 (SHRM 3/4/2001). The survey also revealed that training on ethics increased from one-third in 1994 to 55 per cent in 1999. Another survey of US employees, sponsored by the Society of Financial Service Professionals, reported that almost 90 per cent of respondents claimed that their companies have written codes of ethics and conduct standards. According to the president of the ERC, Micheal Daigneault, 'workplace ethics involves more than just applying the laws and regulations, ethical behaviour refers to standards of conduct such as honesty, fairness, responsibility and trust'. Evidence from the above survey suggests that written ethical codes of conducts have positive impact on employees' behaviour only when top and line managers live by them and set good ethical examples. Otherwise, they build cynicism and scepticism and companies are better off not having them by not demonstrating consistency between their ethical code of conduct and philosophy and ethical behaviour. This is because the ethical conduct of the organization requires the support of the top management.

Nonetheless, Payne and Wayland (1999: 304) noted that HRM is 'still largely relegated to a role of serving strategic and control interests, defined mostly by owners, institutional investors and managers in work organizations, rather than conceived of as a force in helping shape alternative organizational potential'. Consequently, HRM practice 'inhibits the consciousness' of HRM managers towards 'potentially expanding ethical obligations' towards employees. They noted that although HRM managers may accept much of what is found in the ethical codes of professional organizations, such as the IPD and SHRM, in practice, they lack the power and the ethical will to confront a powerful management paradigm geared towards the competitive advantage at any cost. In brief, while the growing desire to make the HRM function more ethical by binding it to a moral code of ethics is understandable, it cannot, we believe, become an ethical function by producing a code of ethics.

HRM AND ETHICS IN PRACTICE

HRM ethical challenges include discrimination, psychological testing, anti-union activity, work design, employment security, employee discipline, confidentiality and employee privacy (Gandtz and Hayes quoted in Payne and Wayland 1999). Danley *et al.*'s survey of over 1000 US HRM professionals reported that the 'most serious ethical situations' US HRM professionals face are: favouritism in hiring, training, promotion, pay and discipline due to friendship with top management; sexual harassment; inconsistent discipline practices; not maintaining confidentiality; sex discrimination in promotion; compensation and recruitment; non-performance factors used in appraisal; and arrangement with vendors or consulting agencies leading to personal gain (quoted in Payne and Wayland 1999: 300).

Ethics and selection

Interviews: Firms widely use employment interviews in the selection process. Different types of interviews are used: structured, semi-structured, focused and unstructured. For many years, academics and practitioners have attempted to develop scientific interviewing techniques to help predict candidate's behaviour, attitudes and efficiency, and therefore select the most appropriate person for the job. It is argued that these techniques will reduce bias and allow interviewees to reach a fair, efficient and objective decision. However, fairness is a vague term and hard to measure especially when interviewing candidates from different ethnic groups and or from cross-cultural backgrounds – members of different ethnic groups or different cultures behave differently during interviews and say things differently. In its narrowest sense, however, fairness refers to choosing a person according to job-related criteria. Whereas choosing, or not choosing, a person because of his or her race, colour, look, gender, nationality and age is generally considered unfair (cf. Arvey and Sackett 1993).

Pearn and Seer (quoted in Spence 2000: 46) suggest the following measures to help avoid such discrimination and unfair recruitment practices:

- Interviews should be properly conducted along professional lines.
- Interviewees should be properly trained.
- Interviewees should be as consistent as possible.
- Interviewees should only be used to assess abilities which cannot be more directly and accurately assessed by other means.

Spence (2000: 55) lists three steps towards 'best ethical practice' in employment interviewing – interviewers should:

- *Step 1.* Acknowledge individual interviewer influence on interviewing and identify actual practices.
- *Step 2.* Understand the reasons for those practices.
- *Step 3.* Clarify and communicate with all participants the preferred ethical stance of the firm.

Psychometric testing: Psychometric tests are often used in the selection process and considered as an 'important component' of the selection event (Baker and Cooper 2000: 61). Baker and Cooper (2000) note that 'the ethics of occupational testing is one area of human resource management where there has already been established ethical debate'. Manese's (1986) book, *Fair and Effective Employment Testing*, highlights several ethical issues facing, and 'best practices' for, occupational testing in the North American context. Since this book was first published, the literature has grown rapidly. Perhaps, this reflects the widespread usage of psychometric testing by Western firms as well, and the manner in which they are deployed. Saville and Holdsworth (1993) note that around 70 per cent of large firms use personality and cognitive measures in their selection process. In some countries such as Sweden, however, there is strong concern about tests and invasion of individual privacy (Baker and Cooper 2000: 61). Advocates of psychometric testing claim that if used properly and in a professional manner it will help the firm predict performance and behaviour of employees better than interviews and other subjective techniques (Cooper and Robertson 1995). According to Baker and Cooper (2000: 60–1), psychometric tests, when used properly, can:

- provide common and neutral language to discuss and understand differences between people
- provide powerful results in a short time span
- offer an idea of strengths and development areas and give a good starting point for open discussion
- provide focus for changing behaviour
- offer people the way to understand themselves better
- generate objective, benchmarked and impartial results (Beardwell and Holden 1997).

However, several articles written by professionals and academics alike have raised concern over the use of psychometric tests in the selection process. These concerns range from employers not following the suggested guidelines of 'good practice' (Baker and Cooper 1985; Commission of Racial Equality, quoted in Baker and Cooper 2000), to the manner in which tests are carried out, and 'fairness, cross-cultural issues and biases of race and gender, test selling practice...types of tests such as integrity and honesty tests, facets of testing practices and testing practices and disabled candidates' (Baker and Cooper 2000: 63). Iles and Robertson (1997) highlight the negative impact of testing on individuals undertaking genetic, integrity, honesty and computer-based tests, because of intrusiveness and their impact on the individual concerned.

Baker and Cooper (2000: 66) note that the changing emphasis in HRM on strategic fit and achieving sustainable competitive advantage has opened a range of new ethical concerns. The testing process not only seeks to predict attitudes and behaviours, but also aims to tell whether the person would fit within the overall corporate strategic vision and structure. Iles and Robertson (1997) argue that, because of the strategic integration of the HRM function and the quest for 'strategic fit', tests have shifted from the traditional job/role and person fit to 'cultural values person fit'. For instance, the results of the tests are widely used to help identify 'core' and 'periphery' workers.

Jackson (1997) reports cases where companies used testing not in a job selection process, but to justify who should go when downsizing takes place. Baker and Cooper (2000: 66) argue that using tests in this way 'is inappropriate because they are measuring constructs that were arguably not genuine occupational or job requirements'. An example would be when existing data input clerks reapplying for similar jobs are rejected on the grounds of not displaying enough 'creativity'.

Baker and Cooper (2000: 68–9) examined testing from a range of different ethical frames of reference and reported the following:

- Utilitarianism: mistakes and negative impact on candidate regrettable, but are acceptable as long as tests have utility for the system as a whole.
- A deontological approach: stresses the regulatory process, and best practices and procedures to avoid harming candidates. A variation of this would be a perspective firmly grounded in Kantian 'universalism': emphasis is placed on testing processes and criteria so tests meet the ethical principle of 'doing unto others as you would have done unto you'.
- Rights-based perspective: stresses egalitarianism, equity, fairness and equity of opportunity.

Ethics and privacy

The right to privacy has been one of the most hotly debated employee rights. Due to technological advances and the way work is conducted in today's world, 'invasion of privacy in the workplace occurs far more frequently than one might expect' (Hartman 1998: 16). Schwoerer *et al.* (1995: 531) argue that because of this 'the protection of employee rights in the workplace is one of the fundamental ethical questions facing organizations today'. The days of employers searching through employees' desks and folders are things of the past. Today, companies collate extensive amount of data on their employees through the use of sophisticated surveillance techniques employing state-of-the-art technology such as closed circuit cameras, monitoring computer use and electronic correspondence, and tapping telephones. A number of employers justify the extensive use of psychometric tests, lie detectors, medical reports and tests – such as drug tests – and the inclusion of day-to-day data in personal records and files, as necessary procedures to create a productive, safe and fair working environment (see Table 6.1). It must be noted that in most cases employees have little or no control over the collation, dissemination and use of such data. The key question is: what can companies monitor to protect themselves without invading employees' 'zone of privacy'? And is any data gathered the firm's property which it can disclose

Table 6.1 Electronic surveillance in the workplace

Videotaping employee activities	15.7%
Reviewing email messages	14.9%
Reviewing computer files	13.7%
Taping telephone conversations	10.4%

Source: American Management Association (www.amanet.org/usindex.htm) (Hartman 1998: 16–20).

it when necessary, or is it a property of the employee, giving her/him the right to full confidentiality? Drawing the line between what is ethical and moral, and what is not, remains one of the most debated and controversial issues in the workplace. Most writers argue that electronic surveillance – especially in private areas such as changing rooms and rest rooms, and the extensive use of polygraph tests or similar tests – is unethical because it violates employees' rights to privacy (Hoffman and Moore 1990). Brenkert (1981) argues that polygraph test are unethical because they violate privacy in two ways. First, through such tests employees give information to employers, which they are not entitled to, such as information on the employee's sex life, past behaviour, medical history, fantasies and so forth, areas that are not directly related to their job performance. Even if the information gathered is directly related to the job at hand, the practice remains unethical because the data is 'obtained by an intrusive method'. Secondly, he argues that polygraph tests are 'notoriously inaccurate and thus run a significant risk of harming honest employees'. Brenkert (quoted in Hoffman and Moore 1990) develops similar arguments against drug tests and other 'intrusive tests and techniques organizations use to "supposedly" improve productivity, and bring absenteeism and labour turn over down'. He argues that organizations should discipline employees for their actions related to their work such as absenteeism, carelessness, low productivity, and not because a test shows a drug metabolite in his or her urine. Put differently, employees are punished, not for *actual* harm or inefficiency but for *potential* harm to the organization. In addition to the above, we argue that it is hard if not impossible to isolate the causes of some of the 'problems' detected by these tests. For instance, a person might have taken drugs because of depression or poverty resulting from not having a job. By giving the person a job we eradicate the cause of the problem. From a legal standpoint, under common law 'unreasonable intrusion into employee's private affair' is prohibited (Hartman 1998). In the United States, common law provides employees with a sphere of privacy as a basic human right. According to Samuel Warren and Louis Brandeis, common law has secured 'to each individual the right of determining, ordinarily, to what extent his thoughts, sentiments, and emotions shall be communicated by others' (Warren and Brandeis 1980). The application of the law on the issue of employees' privacy, however, is 'murky' (Hartman 1998). While employees might argue that monitoring is an invasion of their 'zone of privacy', many employers still contend that monitoring may enhance efficiency, improve productivity, provide safe working environment, enhance customer service and assist them in monitoring employees' performance. Research provides evidence to suggest that monitoring has a direct effect on employees' physical and emotional being. As a result, companies have come under increasing pressure to back off from policies that represent an invasion of privacy or smack of 'spying' on employees (Bylinsky quoted in Schwoerer *et al.* 1995).

Not every one believes that companies should halt their surveillance activities. A survey by the Society of Financial Services Professionals found that only 44 per cent of employees and 33 per cent of employers consider 'monitoring employee email' as an extremely serious or very serious ethical violation. And as little as 32 per cent of employees and 28 per cent of employers consider monitoring employee web-surfing content as extremely serious or very serious ethical violation. Hartman (1998: 16), for example, provides examples and evidence to suggest that companies, under certain circumstances, have the right to monitor email messages to avoid costly lawsuits:

> Employers have a number of reasons to consider monitoring employee email... recently Chevron Corporation... was required to pay four plain-tiffs a total of $2.2 million after their attorneys found evidence of sexual harassment...an email message that had been sent to a number of people within the company containing a list of jokes about 'why beer is better than women (Hartman 1998: 16).

Had Chevron been monitoring its employees' email, he argues, it might have avoided the problem. This line of argument is grounded in utilitarian-ism that it proposes that the greatest good for the greatest number – in this case spying on some to protect the majority – serves as a justification for the ethicality of monitoring employees. Martin (quoted in Hofman and Moore 1990) argues that using the above techniques to monitor employees' activi-ties and restrict their personal liberty is just and fully justifiable. He suggests that because employees are able to move from one job to another, they are able to protect their interests. He claimed that personal liberty at work is not restricted by employers 'tyrannising' employees, but because employee rights are costly, and employees have chosen fewer rights in exchange for higher earning power (Hoffman and Moore 1990: 274). This viewpoint is, of course, grounded in the traditional neo-liberal view of the firm: labour seen as any other commodity, and the employment contract as simply a form of exchange relationship between 'free buyers' and 'sellers'. However, it does not take account of the disproportionate costs of 'exit' – of leaving the job – incurred by most employees compared to the inconvenience suffered by the employer.

Hartman (1998) suggests that if employers decide to monitor their employees, they need to follow the following ethical guidelines:

- There should be no monitoring in highly private areas, such as restrooms.
- Monitoring should be limited to the workplace.
- Employees should have full access to any information gathered through monitoring.
- Continuous monitoring should be banned.

- All forms of secret monitoring should be banned. Employees should always be given advance notice of monitoring.
- Only information relevant to the job should be collected.
- Monitoring should result in the attainment of some business interest.

ETHICAL OBLIGATIONS BETWEEN EMPLOYERS AND EMPLOYEES

Ethics in the workplace is a two-way traffic. The above discussion dealt primarily with obligations of employers towards employees – inter alia, providing meaningful and secure work, fair wages and safe working conditions, privacy, etc. We now focus on potential employee obligations towards employers. From employers' standpoint, employees, or at least core employees, should give their loyalty and commitment to their organization. A key employee moving on to another job imposes many costs on the firm. These include a loss of skills, the possibility that s/he may diffuse critical knowledge and share it with competitors. However, it can be argued that employees have to look after their own careers and long-term welfare in an age of insecure employment contracts. Put differently, how far should employee loyalty go? And are there limits beyond which the demands of loyalty are unreasonable? While it is often assumed that (core) employees should reciprocate when treated ethically by the company, there are many grey areas. What is clear, however, is that certain acts such as sabotage and stealing from the company are simply unethical. A recent survey conducted by the SHRM/Ethics Resource Center found that, during a one-year period, 54 per cent of the 747 US human resource professionals surveyed had observed workplace conduct that broke the law and/or violated the organization's standards of ethical business conduct. The most common was lying to supervisors (45 per cent), abuse of drugs or alcohol (36 per cent), and lying on reports or falsifying records (36 per cent) (see Table 6.2).

In the UK, an MT/KPMG survey of 800 directors on workplace ethics reported that two out of three employees say they lie to their boss (*Management Today* 1/2001). Home office data shows that in 1998–99 there were around 18 000 recorded offences of thefts by employees and more than 1300 of false accounting – see Table 6.3 (*Management Today* 1/2001).

The SHRM/ERC survey reported that 79 per cent of people who observed misconduct reported it to management. People who did not report misconduct listed the following reasons:

- I feared I would be accused of not being a team player   96%
- I didn't believe corrective action would be taken   81%

- I feared retribution or retaliation from my supervisor or management   68%
- Nobody else cares about business ethics, so why should I   58%
- I didn't trust the organization to keep my record confidential   55%
- I feared retribution or retaliation from my co-workers   38%
- It was none of my business   32%
- I didn't know whom to contact   25%
- I didn't want to be known as a whistle blower   20%

Similar findings were reported by the MT/KPMG survey in the UK. Employees stated that they feared reporting on colleagues would alienate them from their peers. Nearly half of the surveyed employees reported that it is not their business to monitor or report violations (see Table 6.4).

Table 6.2 Selected types of ethical misconduct observed

Lying to supervisors	45%
Abusing drugs or alcohol	36%
Lying on reports or falsifying records	36%
Conflicts of interests	34%
Stealing or theft	27%
Receiving gifts/entertainment in violation of organization policy	26%
Misusing organization's assets	24%
Violation of Title VII of the Civil Right Act	23%
Violation of the Fair Labor Standard Act	22%
Altering results of products or service testing	16%
Misusing inside information	14%
Engaging in fraud	12%
Giving gifts in violation of organization policy	10%
Receiving kickbacks	10%
Misusing the organization's proprietary information	10%
Taking bribes	2%

Source: SHRM/ERC Ethics Survey Snapshot (www.shm.org).

Table 6.3 What is and what is not acceptable by employees?

Are these activities acceptable?	
Charging personal entertainment to expenses	2%
Taking sick pay after the office party	6%
Minor fiddling of travel expenses	6%
Favouring family or friends when awarding contracts	6%
Taking software home	15%
Using company petrol for personal mileage	17%
Surfing the net for pleasure in work time	22%
Taking pens and pencils from work	48%
Making personal phone calls from work	75%

Source: MT/KPMG Survey (*Management Today* 1/ 2001: 52).

Table 6.4   Why wouldn't you blow the whistle?

	Men	Women
Alienate myself from my colleagues	21%	26%
Non of my business	49%	40%
Jeopardize my job	13%	18%
Everybody's doing it	30%	42%
It's fair game	5%	5%

Source: Management Today, 2001: 52.

The tables show that while employees recognize that certain acts and attitudes by their fellow employees and/or management are morally impermissible, they considered reporting them as an unacceptable breach of team loyalty or rationalized it by arguing that reporting it does more harm than good especially to themselves.

This leads us to the question: is it ethical to blow the whistle when an employee and/or a manager discovers, or is asked to participate in, an unethical activity? There are two types of whistle blowing. Internal whistle blowing is when the person chooses to reveal the activity to someone higher in the organization. External whistle blowing is when he or she tells someone outside the organization and reveals the activity to a larger external public (Hoffman and Moore 1990). Opinions on whistle blowing vary from one person to another. On one extreme, people such as Ralph Nader recommends that organizations should not punish whistle blowers by firing and/or demoting them, but rather should actively encourage them as a means of improving corporate responsibility (Hoffman and Moore 1990: 275). On the other extreme, some passionately oppose whistle blowing, arguing that it violates the moral and ethical duties of employees to their organization; employees should refrain from such activities. They argue that it could result in the release of confidential information, which could harm the company's competitive position in the market. The chairman of General Motors Corporation, James M. Roche, states that:

> Some of the enemies of business now encourage an employee to be disloyal to the enterprise. They want to create suspicion and disharmony and pry into the proprietary interests of the business: However this is labeled industrial espionage, whistle blowing, or professional responsibility – it is another tactic for spreading disunity and creating conflict (quoted in Hoffman and Moore 1990: 275).

De George (quoted in Hoffman and Moore 1990) argues that because of the potential damage that may occur from whistle blowing, the latter is only morally permissible under certain conditions: the threat of serious physical harm, and after exhausting all other channels within the organization to rectify the situation. He regards it as often unnecessarily 'supererogatory, self sacrificing or heroic', and wherever possible should be avoided.

ETHICS, HRM AND THE LAW

In advanced societies, governments have sought to regulate the way firms manage their human resources for well over a century. This would include health and safety legislation, minimum wage legislation, restrictions as to the length of the working week, and laws protecting the rights of trade unions.

An international trend in labour law over the past 20 years has been towards the paring back of collective employee rights, and the strengthening of the rights of the individual. This reflected the rise of neo-liberal ideologies, the reduced political clout of organized labour, and governments' desire to secure a greater degree of flexibility – above all numerical – and, hence, 'international competitiveness' through the individualization of industrial relations. Nonetheless, despite the conventional wisdom that employee relations have become 'deregulated', there has been a strengthening of the legal rights of employees as individuals. Indeed, whilst the role of trade unions remains contentious, it has been possible to build broad cross-party support for the latter. Whilst strongly in favour of 'deregulation', the neo-liberal orthodoxy remains committed to protecting individual rights, within the rights-based tradition. Meanwhile, more progressive elements would be strongly in favour of any legislation aimed at combating entrenched forms of discrimination. In other words, in these cases, the desire to eliminate discriminatory 'market imperfections' often coincided with pressures to ensure a 'fairer deal' for historically disadvantaged groupings.

In the UK, New Labour's agenda in the field of industrial relations legislation has broadly followed this logic. In short, unions have gained little from most of the legislative changes enacted during the government's tenure. In contrast, the rights of the individual employee have increased, albeit in a somewhat diluted form owing to the government's commitment to a free market. These legislative changes encompass anti-discriminatory measures (most notably on the grounds of gender and race; anti-age discrimination legislation is in the pipeline) and freedom of information measures. Whatever their rationale, recent legislative measures will have the effect of forcing firms to pay more heed to the consequences of their HR policies; HR cannot be solely driven by the bottom line.

SUMMARY

This chapter has examined recent changes in the HRM landscape and how these changes have impacted the management of people in Western organizations. The chapter has shown how the changes in the competitive environment led the rationalization and justification, by management, of previously unacceptable HR practices to make them both plausible and tolerable. The key issues that have dominated and will continue to dominate ethics in HRM are the 'core' and 'periphery' employment and management policies, invasion of employees' privacy and the strategic integration of the HRM function.

KEY QUESTIONS

1. 'Contemporary human resource management accords too little attention to ethical questions'. Critically discuss this statement.
2. What do you think the principal objectives of an ethical code of conduct governing HRM should be?
3. What, do you think, are the principal ethical challenges facing the practice of HRM? Give reasons for your answer.

CASE STUDY: REDUNDANCIES IN A COLD CLIMATE

'A recession, if it comes, will be very different to the last – if you work in the service sector. Redundancy payouts in the media, IT and banking sectors are coming in well above statutory minimums, and mass culls of certain grades of staff, common in the downsizing phenomenon of the early 90s, are out. But in Britain's two-tier economy, manufacturing remains the poor relation when the axe falls on workers.

An example of how the service sector is laying off workers comes from the business magazine division of Reed Elsevier, which publishes titles such as *Farmers Weekly* and *Caterer & Hotelkeeper*.

It has identified five jobs on its motor magazines that it says must go. It says it is now making strenuous efforts to find the people affected jobs on other titles. If that fails, it pays a month's salary for each year worked as part of what it describes as a generous redundancy package. Editorial staff can also expect to receive three months' notice pay.

A spokesman for the company says: "The downturn hit without warning and like most other publishers we have battened down the hatches. But there has always been a generous redundancy package at Reed and we have not seen any reason to change that".

Bradford & Bingley this week said it wanted to cut 500 clerical jobs and create some 200 jobs for financial advisers. But the bank insisted it would ensure that most of the job losses would be voluntary and was keen to encourage existing staff to retrain as financial advisers.

The day before B&B's announcement, Japanese electronics firm Fujitsu said it planned to cut 900 jobs. A spokesman said he expected all the jobs to go through natural wastage, mostly through its DMR manufacturing facility rather than its ICL software and services subsidiary. "Providing IT services is a people business and it is sensible to keep staff on in this area. It is much harder to recruit good staff than it is to retain them".

Simon Webley, a policy adviser at the Institute for Business Ethics, which is funded by about 60 major firms, says the need to keep employees happy through the bad times is important, or they abandon ship when the good times return. "Changes in the law have also pushed companies to behave better", he says. "The changes have signalled that companies cannot just say 'you're out mate' without considering the consequences".

But not everyone – particularly in manufacturing – will be treated with dignity and respect when the job they do is no longer deemed essential by their company.

Peter Booth, national organiser for manufacturing at the Transport & General Union, says little has changed in the way companies in his sector have handled staff relations. He believes manufacturing companies have been largely untouched by the enlightened attitude adopted in other sectors. Most pay the minimum one week's pay for each year worked and give only the minimum notice period.

"Things haven't changed significantly in my day-to-day work. Many companies, especially global companies with subsidiaries in the UK are dealing with huge over capacity in their markets and they react by cutting jobs", he says.

"In the rest of the EU, there are restrictions on withdrawing from a manufacturing facility. The company must draw up a social plan and get agreement with the local council. The council will also want to know if attempts were made to find another buyer. None of this was incorporated into UK law".

"Look at Marks & Spencer. The cuts in stores and jobs it announced in Britain have happened. In France it was forced to go back and think again and instead of the stores simply closing down, they are now up for sale with the prospect that there might be a buyer and the jobs saved".

Steel maker Corus shocked staff and unions when it told shareholders that 5,000 jobs and several plants would close. It was a shoot first, think later policy that encapsulated the worst aspects of cutbacks in manufacturing.

Yet the threat of an appearance at an industrial tribunal for breaching laws incorporated from EU directives has persuaded many employers that being nice pays.

Meriel Schindler, head of employment law at solicitors Withers, says investment banks in the City are a case in point. Many instituted job freezes at the beginning of the year. Then came job cuts. The hardest hit have been staff at subsidiaries of the giant US banks such as Merrill Lynch and Goldman Sachs.

But the banks have tried to stop themselves from over-reacting to what could be a brief downturn in work. Many have adopted voluntary redundancy programmes. Others have paid staff more than they were expecting in severance pay. Several have done both.

Public relations companies and firms of headhunters have been hit by budget cuts in the City and, in Ms Schindler's experience, have mostly approached the prospect of job cuts in the same way:

"The companies we come into contact with are starting to deal with the situation with more caution and more sensitivity. It is fair to say that every human resources department knows that unfairly dismissing someone is no longer a cheap way to get rid of them".

A survey by consultants Penna Sanders and Sidney goes some way to supporting the idea that employers have improved. More than a third (37%) agreed that employers have a more responsible attitude towards redundancy. Only a fifth disagreed.

The sensitivity and caution are largely borne of fear that a redundancy programme will end up as an acrimonious court case.

Staff have for some time been able to claim that their redundancy is, in fact, unfair dismissal. But until three years ago the most compensation someone could win was £11,000. Few people bothered to complain given the paltry sums on offer. The Labour government increased the figure to £50,000. It now stands at £51,000.

The number of complaints has trebled in the last three years to 130,000, which the Confederation of British Industry says shows the new laws have gone too far. This week it claimed employment tribunals, many of them concerned with cases of unfair dismissal following a redundancy programme, will cost businesses £633m in 2001, up from £426m in 1999.

Digby Jones, director general of the CBI, said employers were seeing their consultation and dispute procedures bypassed by employees who went straight to tribunals to win compensation payments:

"In too many cases the tribunal system is the solution of first resort rather than last resort. That is bad for employers but it is also bad for employees who face a stressful court case and often find themselves out of a job or in lower paying work", he says.

The TUC said many firms involved in disputes had failed to draw up procedures that allow someone to complain. Small firms are the most likely to ignore procedures and even laws when they announce redundancies, though many laws only apply to larger companies.

Worst off are the workers at companies which go bust rather than slimming down. When the receivers march in, they only pay the legal minimum redundancy and there is no chance of ex-gratia payments to soften the blow.

Another tactic is to worsen employees' terms and conditions to avoid redundancy. Workers at car maker Rover, for example, have seen their pay cut and their pension entitlements reduced in order to keep the firm solvent. While in this case it was openly negotiated with the workforce, many other firms use it as a tactic to cut costs in a downturn regardless of their financial position.

Mr Booth says one firm in North Wales asked its staff for cuts in pay, holidays and a host of other entitlements. The workforce refused to agree. They were locked out of the factory and after the legal consultation period was over they were all sacked. These are extreme examples, but they show that while service industries that count people as their key resource are being fairer, many manufacturers still consider their staff a commodity to be used and abused.

Perhaps they should take heed of a growing trend in the US, where firms that have treated staff like they would steal paperclips have reported a huge growth in sabotage by those made redundant. Emailing a computer virus or three to their former employer is a particularly popular pastime among disgruntled sacked staff. That's another reason to use redundancy as a last resort' (*Guardian* 25/8/2001).

ISSUES

In your opinion, what is the best way to deal with 'over capacity' when firms face a slow down? Do you think it is right to continuously adjust and readjust employment policies to market downturns by hiring–firing and rehiring tactics?

FURTHER READING

Danely, J., Harrick, E., Strickland, D. and Sullivan, G. 1991. 'HR ethical situation', *Human Resource Management*, 26 June: 1–12. Although slightly dated, this article provides a good introduction to the topic.

Legge, K. 1998. 'Is HRM ethical? Can HRM be ethical?', in Parker, M. (ed.), *Ethics and Organizations*. London: Sage. This chapter critically examines the relative morality of HRM.

Winstanley, D., and Woodall, J. (eds). 2000. *Ethical Issues in Contemporary Human Resource Management*. London: Macmillan. This edited volume provides a comprehensive coverage of most ethical challenges facing HRM.

ETHICS, ACCOUNTING AND FINANCE

As shocking as the Enron fiasco is, it is only the latest in a dizzying succession of accounting meltdowns, from Waste Management to Cendant. Auditors have always been in the uncomfortable position of having to judge the financial integrity of the companies that pay them. But in the fast-moving 1990s, with intensifying pressure to produce ever rising earnings and stock prices, Corporate America began to push the accounting boundaries like never before. And auditors were thrust into a new role of enabler. The accounting industry, which largely regulates itself, has steadfastly resisted change, even in the face of repeated audit failures and scandals. That is about to change. The size and scope of the Enron disaster is simply too huge to ignore ('Accounting in crisis', *Business Week*, January 28, 2002: 44).

This chapter discusses business ethics in finance and accounting. Intensified competition on a global basis, together with radical changes in the accounting profession (Lawrence, 1998), such as the rise of 'creative accounting', have raised a number of well-publicized moral dilemmas for financial analysts and accountants. Finn *et al.* (1994: 27) argue that many accountants believe 'unethical behaviour is on the increase' and that 'incentives and pressures in the marketplace may lead to even more widespread use of unethical behaviour to secure and retain clients'. Not so well-publicized ethical concerns that, but no less important, are the conflicts of values that arise for financiers and accountants.

The chapter is divided into three parts. The first part looks at recent changes in financial management practices. The second part deals with ethical financial practices – financial code ethics and how they are enforced, or not, in practice. The third part analyses the ethicality of current financial and accounting management practices.

ETHICS AND FINANCIAL MANAGEMENT

Dobson (1997) argues that 'it would be an understatement' to claim that the disciplines of ethics and finance have not been strongly associated with each other. According to Dobson the two disciplines 'have been opposed to each other as mutually exclusive'. The latter is a result of several intertwined factors acting together. A number of writers examined moral dilemmas facing financial analysts and accountants. Drummond and Bain (1994: 185) state that 'anyone taking serious interest in ethics of business quickly comes to the conclusion that accountants have a key, if not a central, role to play'. This role, however, 'is becoming increasingly controversial'. Similarly, Jack (1994: 186) notes:

> Ask a group of customers whether business has ethics and they are likely to laugh in derision. Ask a group of business executives the same about accountants, and the answer is not likely to be so different.

One of the primary reasons for ethical concerns over financial and accounting practices is the fact that practitioners of management accounting and financial management on the one hand have an obligation to the public and the state, and on the other hand to the organization or clients they serve. Dobson (1997) argues that 'the ethics of finance is underdeveloped compared to the fields of business ethics or professional ethics' because 'most financiers have not had a strong ethical formation', whereas ethicists 'lack an understanding of the technicality of financial management, and thus the situation perpetuates itself'.

Another cause of growing ethical concerns in finance and accounting is the aggressive competitive environment and changes in the role of the profession. A survey by The Ethics Resource Center/Society for Human Resource Management (1997) in the United States showed that 'meeting overly aggressive financial or business objectives' as the principal cause of ethical compromise. Activities that may undermine the integrity of the financial accountant include, schemes to overstate a company's earnings and financial condition, wilfully and extensively falsifying corporate records, lying to auditors, coercing vendors into covering up practices, improperly applying accounting principles, making false disclosures, and repeatedly violating general accepted accounting principles.

In the United States, accountants and financiers claim that the accounting profession has been perceived by the public as being among the more ethical of business professions. Warth (2000: 69) notes that 'CPAs' high ethical standards are the foundation for their trust in the mind of the public'. This is because the accounting profession has been founded on the notion that proper ethical behaviour is a cornerstone of providing professional services to the client (Finn *et al.* 1994). These ethical behaviours are enforced by professional ethical codes of conducts that every accountant and financier must adhere to as a condition for membership to professional organizations. Advocates of codes of ethics in finance and accounting argue that they are beneficial as a guide to professional conduct, and as a basis for making judgements with respect to ethical dilemmas. For instance, CPAs who violate the code are subject to sanctions and the loss of licence. Cottell and Perlin (1990: 18) assert that one of the defining characteristics of a professions is '(t)he capacity to regulate itself, often with the sanction of the law for those who violate acceptable norms of behaviour'.

Several researchers have explored the merits and demerits of strict ethical codes and standards that rely primarily on enforcement of procedures, and punishment in case of non-adherence, or a laissez-faire approach based on moral and ethical training to motivate accountants to behave morally without institutional monitoring (see Barry 1999). Advocates of the latter argue that accounting and finance practitioners like other professionals should be left free to apply their skills, expertise and seasoned judgement, guided by moral conscience and not by rigid rules and regulations. Advocates of the former approach, however, further question the application of accounting and finance codes of ethics: are they legalistic documents – prescriptive – and therefore adhering to the codes is suffice for claiming that the practice is ethical? The jury is still out on the latter question, but in practice, it is observed that although the accounting and finance codes of practice may be described as rather prescriptive, accountants have generally discouraged a legalistic reading. Put differently, accountants and financiers are expected to abide by the spirit of the code and the professional ethic it prescribes. For example, in the 1977 report by the Subcommittee on Reports,

Accounting and Management of the Committee on Governmental Affairs, US Senate, the subcommittee stated:

> ...(it) agrees that disciplinary actions should be expedited, and should be based on failure to follow high professional standards, rather than violation of legal standards (US Congress 1977).

An ethical violation may be either a violation of a legal requirement or presentation of accounting information that may be misleading to potential users of financial information (Beckman *et al.* 1989). In the performance of their duties, accountants are expected to adhere to personal standards that go beyond legal formalities. The Institute of Management Accounting (IMA) (Strategic Finance Editors 1999) listed five acts that practitioners of management accounting and finance have to adhere to:

- *Competence.* Practitioners of management accounting and financial management have the responsibility to maintain appropriate levels of professional competence; perform their professional duties in accordance with relevant laws, regulations, and technical standards; prepare complete and clear reports and recommendations after appropriate analysis of relevant and reliable information.
- *Confidentiality.* They should refrain from disclosing confidential information acquired during the course of their work; inform subordinates as appropriate regarding the confidentiality of information acquired in the course of their work and monitor their activities to ensure the maintenance of that confidentiality; refrain from using or appearing to use confidential information acquired in the course of their work for unethical or illegal advantages either personally or through third parties.
- *Integrity.* They have the responsibility to avoid actual or apparent conflicts of interests and advise all appropriate parties of any potential conflict; refrain from engaging in any activity that would prejudice their ability to carry out their duties ethically; refuse any gift, favour, or hospitality that would influence or would appear to influence their actions; refrain from either actively or passively subverting the attainment of the organization's legitimate and ethical objectives; recognize and communicate professional limitations or other constraints that would preclude responsible judgement or successful performance of an activity; communicate unfavourable as well as favourable information and professional judgements or opinions; and refrain from engaging in or supporting any activity that would discredit the profession.
- *Objectivity.* They are responsible to communicate information fairly and objectively; and disclose fully all relevant information that could reasonably be expected to influence an intended user's understanding of the reports, comments, and recommendations presented.

- *Resolution of ethical conflict.* When faced with significant ethical issue, they should follow the established policies of the organization bearing on the resolution of the conflict. If the latter do not resolve the ethical conflict, they should consider the following courses of action: discuss the issue with immediate superior, if the issue is not resolved, submit the issue to the next higher management level or other relevant internal bodies. (For more details see Strategic Finance Editors 1999).

It must be mentioned that ethical standards are not static but evolve as the business, economic, technological and social contexts within which they operate change (we will explore this point in more detail later). For instance, the US accounting profession has continued to monitor, revise and update its professional standards. In the late 1980s, the American Institute of CPAs (AICPA) conducted extensive revisions and adopted a revised Code of Professional Conduct (American Institute of Certified Public Accountants 1988; Anderson 1985; Anderson and Ellyson 1986; Shaub 1988). These revisions were sparked off by a US congressional investigation of the accounting profession, which proposed legislation that would regulate the profession if it proved incapable of demonstrating more active self-regulation efforts. The above investigation revealed concerns by representatives of business and industry that the standards of ethical conduct for CPAs were not providing sufficient guidance for accounting professionals (see Graber 1979). In the revised code, the AICPA specified a set of general rules governing conduct as well as proper ethical behaviour for CPAs.

THE ACCOUNTING PROFESSION: PUSHING THE BOUNDARIES OF ETHICS?

This is largely an empirical question, but so far little empirical research has been done to resolve it in one way or another (see Finn *et al.* 1994). There is, however, a large body of anecdotal evidence that seems to support an affirmative answer. Finn *et al.* (1994: 27) found that CPAs could be grouped into two groups. The first group consists of those who believe that unethical behaviour is already widespread and that there are few, if any, deterrents to a continued growth of such unethical practices. They believed that the profession was ineffective in enforcing ethical standards, and that the partners of the CPA firms were similarly lax in enforcing ethical standards within their firms. They reported that some CPAs believed that unethical behaviour was condoned and could actually improve one's opportunity for advancement in the profession (Finn *et al.* 1998). The second group held a more positive view of ethical conduct. They believed that 'while unethical behaviour is not yet widespread, competitive pressures have led to an increase in unethical behaviour'. Understandably, the latter group called for tighter policing and reprimanding CPAs that did not comply with ethical standards.

CREATIVE ACCOUNTING AND ETHICS

Prior to the 1980s, the caricature of an accountant was someone who was cautious, backward-looking, wore grey, unimaginative, boring and had no sense of humour. Thanks to the changing nature of the equity market in the 1980s, the profession has changed beyond recognition. It led to the birth of creative accounting, which is widely practised by both large and small companies (Shah 1996; Paterson 1995). Creative accounting is here to stay because 'no amount of legislation, no code of best practice, and no system of accounting standards' can get rid of it (Pijper 1994). In simple terms, creative accounting is the use of permitted cosmetic window dressing accounting techniques to present a flattering picture of a company's financial state. In some cases, creative accounting techniques are used to create a false impression while providing information that is not, in itself, untruthful (For an extensive review of how creative accounting produces misleading information using real-life examples see Pijper 1994.) Howard (1996) states that creative accounting is 'an example of hiding the truth while sticking assiduously to the rules'. It reflects pressure from executives who wish to create the impression of enhancing profitability and strengthening the balance sheet to ensure a healthy demand for shares (Whittington *et al.* 1995). The latter would subsequently reduce the need for external borrowing, and help justify strategic moves such as acquisitions and/or defence against hostile take-overs. The accounting and finance profession responded by a development of a wide range of creative techniques, 'which broke with the caution of the past and seemed to spurn a predominant emphasis on the true underlying financial position of the company' (Jack 1984: 186–7). A well-publicized example is the technique that was used by the Polly Peck Group (see Howard 1996). It is alleged that 'the company borrowed in Swiss francs at an apparently low interest rate, but Swiss franc appreciation against sterling meant that the real sterling cost of borrowing was much higher'. A 'loophole in accounting rules allowed this huge extra cost to be ignored in calculating the company's profit, which was made to look much greater' (Howard 1996: 66).

Creative accounting is not always used to exaggerate profit. Sometimes it used to minimize profit or show a fictitious loss. Munk (1995) cites the example of Paramount Pictures' movie, *Forrest Gump*, which was made to appear – thanks to creative accounting – to make a loss rather than a profit despite taking over $657 million at box office around the world. As a result some parties in the movie-making process who were entitled to a portion of the net profit did not get their fair share.

In the UK, creative accounting has been challenged by critics who describe it as 'fiddling with profits' (Griffiths 1986), 'manipulation, deceit and misrepresentation' (Jameson 1988), an 'accounting sleight of hand' (Smith 1992), and potential 'abuse' (Naser 1993). However, Breton and Taffler (1995), using a laboratory experiment in which a large sample of experienced investment analysts participated, found that creative accounting was not viewed as a serious problem. They stated that contrary to conventional wisdom, there is little evidence of window dressing adjustments made by the subject – creative accounting – in general.

Creative accounting has also led to the rise of 'opinion shopping' by companies searching for preferable ways of presenting their financial status. This could lead to a situation where companies select those accountants, accounting firms and financiers to produce their reports that have the reputation of being sympathetic to certain irregularities, the notorious being well-known financial 'beauty therapists'. In such an environment, financiers and accountants with a strong ethic will find it hard to attract and retain clients.

Century Business Services Incorporated represents a widely cited example of unethical practices due to creative accounting (*Business Week* 2000). This public-held company expanded into the seventh-largest US accounting firm by acquiring small and medium sized firms. The company's reported revenues nearly tripled in 1977, and they doubled in 1988 (*Business Week* 2000). But the company came under heavy criticism for controversial reporting methods that inflated its earnings. Critics claimed that, for example, some of the company's earnings were misrepresented, by being based on projected rather than actual (historical) growth. Other accusations included the vending of artificially inflated shares, and at least in one case, the company accounted for an acquisition before the deal was technically closed. After advice from the Securities & Exchange Commission, net income was reduced in 2000 by $16 million (*Business Week* 2000). Accusations and controversies over its financial reporting methods resulted in a sharp fall in the price of Century shares. Although the company sought to revise its reporting methods and started reporting much lower expected income, share prices continued to fall. And the company's chief operating officer resigned after a downward revision of the 2000 forecast. This case is of extreme significance – an accounting firm having problems over its own accounting system. The case of Century is an example of aggressive use of creative accounting that patently went wrong (*Business Week* 2000).

Michael Josephson (Buckics 1999), president of the Josephson Institute of Ethics lists the following as the principal causal factors in the elevation of ethical concerns in accounting to new heights:

- environmental problems
- the impact of technology
- the increasing use of numerical goals as the standard measure of success
- the global nature of the business environment, which results in increased systems design and auditing responsibilities.

SUMMARY

As a response to recent changes in the business environment, the accounting and financial profession has changed itself beyond recognition. It has moved from mere reporter of facts relating to the financial health of the company to a management tool that could be misused to project a different financial reality. In turn, the latter has fuelled concern over the ethicality of certain 'deceptive but legal' practices. Two schools of thought have emerged. The first one advocates that financial and accounting codes of ethics are essential to maintain and enforce ethical practices, and strongly supports rigid but effective codes of ethics that all accountants and financiers should adhere to. The second school argues that 'straitjacket' laws and regulations cannot regulate the function. The latter, it is argued, will create a culture where accountants and financiers will adhere to the minimum required by a code of ethics that cannot cover all possible ethical issues. Thus, accounting professionals should be self-regulated. However, this viewpoint has become increasingly untenable in the face of repeated financial scandals: accounting is perhaps a too serious business to be left to the discretion of accountants.

KEY QUESTIONS

1. 'By branching out into consulting, accounting firms have hopelessly compromised the traditional role of the auditor'. Critically discuss this statement.
2. 'Creative accounting is unethical and should face the strongest legal sanctions'. Critically discuss this statement.
3. Do you think the Institute of Management's five principles (or 'Acts') that practitioners of management accounting and finance have to adhere to are sufficient to ensure ethical conduct? Give reasons for your answer.

CASE STUDY: MONITORING FINANCIAL AND SOCIAL CONDUCT

'The Co-operative Bank has long been regarded as outside the mainstream when it comes to deciding to whom it will lend and how it will conduct its business. Now it has updated its ethical policy in a move that it believes will keep the bank at the forefront of the issue until well into the next century.

Simon Williams, the bank's head of corporate affairs, says the review, announced at the turn of the year, was an essential part of ensuring that the Co-op's policy "echoes developments in society at large".

He adds: "We are committed to regularly consulting our customers on the details of our ethical stance. After all, it is their money in the bank. New ethical concerns arise from time to time, and if they involve a question of finance or banking, they will be put before our customers. We then adopt a stance on these issues if our account holders mandate us to do so".

The biggest change to the policy involves extending the bank's ecological commitments to business activities considered unsustainable. As a result, the bank will not invest in companies whose core activity relies on the extraction or production of fossil fuels, the manufacture of unnatural chemicals or the "unsustainable harvest of natural resources". Revisions have also been made to the stance on the arms trade, human rights and trade and social involvement.

In particular, the bank is seeking to use its influence in the development of the "social economy" through assisting co-ops, credit unions and charities. Already 60 per cent of credit unions bank with the Co-op.

Other organisations are also promoting the importance of social and ethical accounting. In the autumn the New Economics Foundation published the "quality scoring framework", with the aim of allowing the comparison and evaluation of different approaches to social accountability. And this week the Institute of Social and Ethical Accountability hosts a conference on "the practice of social reporting for business".

The event, to be held at the Commonwealth Conference Centre in London on 19 January, will include presentations from Paul Monaghan, partnership development manager at the Co-op, Chris Tuppen, social and environmental measurement manager at BT, and John Elkington, chairman of the SustainAbility consultancy.

The organisers say: "Business and corporate success can no longer be defined solely in terms of earnings, growth and the balance sheet as social and ethical responsibility has become both an individual necessity and an organisational requirement".

> The Co-op is confident that it is in a good position to encourage those who do not see how matters are developing. "Every company needs a bank account and many need lines of finance. Therefore, a bank is in a strong position to decide whether to fund a business activity or not", says Mr Williams' (*Independent* 17/1/01).

ISSUES
....

What role, if any, do you think, banks have in ensuring ethical behaviour by their clients? And, should the definition of auditing be expanded to encompass not only the monitoring of financial procedures and conduct, but also, social ones?

FURTHER READING
....

Dobson, J. 1997. *Finance Ethics: The Rationality of Virtue.* Oxford: Rowman and Littlefield. One of the few general books published on this area.

Naser, K. 1993. *Creative Financial Accounting: Its Nature and Use.* London: Prentice-Hall. It critically examines the ethicality of creative accounting.

Smith, T. 1992. *Accounting for Growth.* London: Prentice-Hall. A controversial book. It provides an insider's view into the misuse of creative accounting in business practices.

ETHICS AND SUPPLY CHAIN MANAGEMENT

CHAPTER OUTLINE
....

Comprehending ethical supply chain management
Current ethical challenges in supply chain management
  Ethics and purchasing: gifts and gratuities
The supply chain and the fair treatment of labour
Greening the supply chain

Within the general supply chain management, an increasing emphasis has been placed on the need for ethical issues to be taken seriously. However, much of the debate surrounding business ethics still accords insufficient attention to the different partners in the supply chain and their willingness and ability, or lack of them, to actively manage their business ethically. In particular, one question is crucial: are companies responsible for the actions of their suppliers and distributors? Furthermore, it is unclear that the ethical role of the 'main' firms in the supply chain can be easily reconciled within the supply chain.

The purpose of this chapter is to identify the key ethical areas in supply chain management, to examine their challenges and controversies in terms of monitoring suppliers and purchasers, and to consider whether their unethical management practices anywhere along the chain can be altered by the main firm, such that a more proactive ethical role by the firm becomes worth while. This chapter is structured as follows. The first section provides a brief summary of the concept of supply chain management. The second section gives a general overview of the key ethical areas in supply chain management. The third section examines current issues, such as the greening of the supply chain, and supply chain and the sweat shop.

COMPREHENDING ETHICAL SUPPLY CHAIN MANAGEMENT

There seems to be a universal agreement on what a supply chain is. Quite simply, the supply chain is the all-inclusive set including linkages from raw materials to end-customers. Supply chain management is the oversight of materials, information and finances as they move in a process from supplier to manufacturer to wholesaler to retailer to consumer. It involves coordinating and integrating these flows both within and among companies. Janyashankar *et al.* (1996) defines a supply chain as 'a network of autonomous or semi-autonomous business entities collectively responsible for procurement, manufacturing, and distribution activities associated with one or more families of related products'. Lee and Billington (1995) provide a similar definition:

> A supply chain is a network of facilities that procure raw materials, transform them into intermediate goods and then final products, and deliver the products to customers through a distribution system.

In brief, supply chain management is the processes from initial raw materials to the ultimate consumption of the finished product, linking across supplier–user companies. In this sense, the supply chain is the organizational crystallization of real material flows that form the life cycle of the product from the cradle to the grave (Green *et al.* 2000). When a supply chain cuts across national boundaries, and is primarily concerned with the movement of raw or semi-processed commodities, it is sometimes referred to as a global commodity chain (GCC). Here, producers of primary commodities, intermediaries and buyers constitute part of an effective global organization (Sklair 1995: 62). GCCs are dealt with in greater depth in Chapter 5.

Supply chain management comprises the business processes that bring a product or service to market, including coordination, communication and collaboration among suppliers; manufacturing, materials, transportation and warehouse management; and procurement, distribution, wholesale and service and sales channels. Organizations achieve supply chain excellence by breaking organizational barriers through close communication, coordination and collaboration with their suppliers, enabling visibility into the supply chain viewing and monitoring the activities of the supply chain's effectiveness, and managing through breaking organizational barriers and enabling collaboration across the supply chain.

The central aim of ethical supply chain management is to have the right products in the right quantities (at the right place) at the right moment at minimal cost, translated into the interrelated issues of customer satisfaction, inventory management and flexibility within an ethical framework. Customer satisfaction is to a high degree dependent on the flexibility of the supply chain, that is its ability to respond to changes in demand. Flexibility is often imperfect because of long lead times, uncertainties and unforeseen events. To counterbalance this lack of flexibility, companies will keep inventories at various levels of the supply chain. Balancing the costs of imperfect customer satisfaction and holding inventory is a classic issue of logistics and supply chain management.

Slack *et al.* (2001) noted that operations management strategies must be ethical as there are ethical implications in almost every decision in the area of operations management. As manufacturing firms outsource more parts and services to focus on their own core competencies, they increasingly expect their suppliers to deliver innovative and quality products on time and at a competitive cost. As a result, managing the supply chain has become key to achieving sustainable competitive advantage. Logistics can no longer be narrowly defined from an internally focused perspective, but from a holistic one taking all the supply chain into consideration. But how responsible is the company for those parts of the supply chain that are outside of its physical boundaries? In this chapter, we argue that although it is difficult, maintaining ethical standards throughout the supply chain is an important ethical cornerstone. For instance, anecdotal evidence in the popular media seem to suggest that ethical behaviour in the food and grocery logistics supply chain has been on the decline for a long time. Unfortunately, this topic is brushed aside and silenced because each participant in the chain is afraid 'whistle blowing' will lose them business.

The strategic supply chain alignment literature advocates that firms should improve relationships between markets, strategy, culture and leadership throughout the supply chain. The better the alignment, including the ethical standards, the better the bottom-line performance. Slack *et al.* (2001)

note that some of the ethical issues in the supply chain include: honesty in supplier relationships, transparency of cost data, non-exploitation of developing country suppliers, prompt payment to suppliers, minimizing energy consumption in distribution, and greening the supply chain.

CURRENT ETHICAL CHALLENGES IN SUPPLY CHAIN MANAGEMENT

This section first outlines the key ethical challenges and problems in supply chain management which may be expected to give rise to conditions where the firm has to expand its governance to maintain an ethical standard throughout the supply chain.

Carter (2000) notes that in the current competitive business environment, pressures to increase sales on the outbound side and to lower costs and improve supplier performance on the inbound side continue to rise. Carter quotes a respondent as saying: 'As companies are pushing for improved performance, people will take greater risks and push the envelope…. the fear of losing your job is great'. Consequently, purchasing managers under strong pressure to deliver may, for example, be more likely to engage in unethical practices such as using obscure contract terms or exaggerating the seriousness of a problem when doing business with a supplier, in order to gain price concessions and meet performance goals and expectations (Carter 2000). Cooper *et al.* (1997) argue that the three most common ethical violations in purchasing are showing partiality towards suppliers preferred by upper management, a failure to provide products and services of the highest quality in the eyes of the internal customers, and receiving gifts or entertainment that influence, or appear, to influence purchasing decisions.

However, given the fact that the purchasing and sales functions are boundary-spanning functions, and have significant influence on how other members of the supply chain network view a firm, ethical attitudes in purchase and sales are imperative. Furthermore, because sales and purchasing functions are exposed to a firm's external environment, they may be under even greater pressure than other internal functions to deviate from the firm's accepted norms of behaviour (Ferrel and Gresham 1985).

It is often argued that effectively communicating ethics policies to suppliers may act as a deterrent to purchasing personnel tempted to act in an unethical manner. However, as we have argued throughout this book behavioural standards, such as a code of ethics, without associated sanctions are really just window dressing. Appropriate and enforced sanctions might not only positively affect the behaviour of purchasing personnel, but also serve to demonstrate to those outside purchasing, including suppliers, that the company really cares, or not as the case may be, about.

Ethics and purchasing: gifts and gratuities

It has long been recognized that in business there is no such thing as a free lunch. In purchasing, it is considered as a device that facilitates preferential treatments of some suppliers and/or buyers (Turner *et al.* 1994; Rudelius and Buchholz 1997), or to put pressure on the buying firm to reciprocate. Turner *et al.* (1994) found that the acceptance of gratuities by purchasing people is a significant concern of those in the profession as well as upper management. Acceptance of gifts or gratuities has been forbidden by most professional associations, such as the American National Association of Purchasing Management (NAPM). Consequently, several (mostly large) companies have taken a proactive policy and developed a company policy that forbids the acceptance of gratuities and gifts (see NAPM principles below). Cummings (1979) argues, however, that purchasing in many firms continues to be dominated by 'do-as-I-say-not-as-I-do' attitudes. The latter is a result of double standards attitudes in several companies as they often reprimand buyers for accepting gifts or favours from suppliers, yet reward sales staff for their use of such 'sharp practice' in order to secure new contracts and accounts.

The NAPM Principles and Standards of Purchasing Practice refers to the ethical problems associated with accepting gifts in a number of its passages. Here are just two such examples:

- Avoid the intent and appearance of unethical or compromising practice in relationships, actions, and communications.
- Refrain from soliciting or accepting money, loans, credits, or prejudicial discounts, and the acceptance of gifts, entertainment, favours, or services from present or potential suppliers that might influence, or appear to influence, purchasing decisions.

It is worth noting, however, that the new buyer–supplier paradigm is based on alliances (Heide and John 1990) and partnership (Anderson and Narus 1990), and, as such is fundamentally different from the traditional, often adversarial, buyer–supplier relationships. In the former, buyers and suppliers work together to create a boundaryless (Ashkenas 1990) relationship. The new supplier–buyer paradigm makes preferential treatment not only acceptable but also desirable. This paradigm makes it very difficult for firms to distinguish between actions, attitudes and behaviours aiming at strengthening the relationship – which are desirable – or putting pressure on the buying department to reciprocate or give preferential treatments.

GM'S POLICY COVERING GIFTS, ENTERTAINMENT AND OTHER GRATUITIES FROM SUPPLIERS

....

Both as a matter of sound procurement practice and basic business integrity, we at General Motors must make our purchase decisions solely on the basis of which suppliers offer General Motors the best value for the goods and services we need. We should avoid doing anything that suggests our purchase decisions may be influenced by any irrelevant or improper consideration whether illegal, such as a kickback or bribe, or technically legal, such as personal friendship, favors, gifts or entertainment.

Consequently, it is General Motors policy that no General Motors employee accept any gift, entertainment or other gratuity from any supplier to General Motors or bidder for General Motors business, including supplier units which are part of General Motors. This policy applies to all employees whether or not they are directly involved in purchasing activities.

There may be rare circumstances where to refuse a gift conceivably could be against General Motors' legitimate business interests, particularly in those countries where gift giving is simply an expected social courtesy and is not intended to corrupt or influence a particular purchase decision. There inevitably will be gray areas or situations where the applicability of this policy may not be immediately apparent. For example, very inexpensive mementoes, such as 'logo' pens, cups, caps, or other similar items of nominal value, may be accepted subject to any more stringent policy which your business unit may adopt.

To help in interpreting this policy, several illustrations of its application to hypothetical fact situations are attached. In the final analysis, however, the best course is to decline any gift, entertainment or other gratuity from a supplier to General Motors. Any questionable situation should be discussed with your supervisor to determine how best to handle it. If there is a reason for you ever to accept a particular gift of any real value, it should be reported to your management and the gift always must be turned over to the Corporation for display, use or other appropriate disposition (Anonymous 1996).

Turner *et al.* (1995) note that, because of the increased emphasis on building and maintaining long-term cooperative relationships, an ethical purchasing function is imperative for the development of a relationship based on mutual trust (see Barath and Hugstad 1977). Marucheck and Robins (1998) assert that the trust-based relationship within the supply chain is imperative in the current, highly competitive, business environment. They argue that an ethical purchasing function is a necessary condition for the success of, for instance, just-in-time (JIT) purchasing practice. Within a JIT strategy, the buyer minimizes its inventories by relying on the supplier to deliver the needed goods or services just in time for processing. The fragility of the system requires total trust and reliance on ethical behaviour from all parties involved.

THE SUPPLY CHAIN AND THE FAIR TREATMENT OF LABOUR

Through the past decades we have seen an increasing rate of globalization of the economy and thereby also of supply chains. Products are no longer produced and consumed within the same geographical area. Even the different parts of a product may, and often do, come from all over the world. This creates longer and more complex supply chains, and therefore it also changes the requirements within supply chain management.

As a result of the intense global competition in Western countries, firms are increasingly relying on international sourcing in most cases to reduce costs and sustain their competitiveness (Monczka and Trent 1991). One of the main ethical challenges for firms outsourcing internationally is the maintenance of labour conditions that are legal and acceptable to Western customers. One of these challenges is the 'sweatshop' issue. There is no short supply of stories and anecdotal evidence in the popular media, below are some of the examples:

- Thai 'slave labourers' sewing fashions for major department stores in the Los Angeles suburb of El Monte.
- Haitian workers earning six cents for every '101 Dalmatians' outfit that Disney sells for $20.
- Children in maquiladoras in Honduras and women in sweatshops in New York City sewing clothes for Wal-Mart's Kathie Lee Gifford label.
- Guess, the highly profitable designer-jeans company, failing to live up to an agreement to stop sweat shop conditions among its contractors in Los Angeles, then firing union supporters and shifting production to Mexico to thwart a union organizational drive.
- The use of child labour in Pakistan in the production of footballs by suppliers for the FIFA.

In the United States, in theory, firms found guilty of handling merchandise produced in sweatshops would be subject to federal sanctions for violating the 'hot goods' provisions of the 1983 Fair Labour Standards Act (Lewis 1994). In 1997, legislation was proposed by Congress that would hold manufacturers and retailers liable for human right abuses by their contractors (US Congress 1997). Because of these concerns, in 1996, the so-called Apparel Industry Partnership (AIP) was formed under the auspices of President Clinton (Harris and Mckay 1997). In 1997 the AIP produced the 'workplace code of conduct' action plan and recommendations for monitoring suppliers to ensure that stipulations contained in the code were being adhered to (Blustein 1997). In similar vein, the Council on Economic Priority (CEP), a New York-based public interest group, established a new quality of work life standard known as Social Accountability 8000 (SA8000) (Berstein 1997). The latter is intended to serve as a benchmark to ensure that international suppliers conform to recognized standards pertaining to the use of child labour, the working environment, wages and collective bargaining rights. In brief, companies need to ensure that goods and services are produced and distributed under humane, equitable conditions, even though suppliers are outside the company's physical arena (Berstein 1997). Differences in defining what is meant by child labour, however, vary from one country and region to another.

Emmelhainz and Adams (1999) note that monitoring overseas suppliers involves three tasks. First, a 'code of conduct' specifying standards of employee welfare which suppliers are expected to adhere to. The latter should be communicated to all affected parties in the supply chain. Second, a monitoring system to make sure that suppliers comply with agreed-upon ethical standards. The latter could take the form of visits, inspections, interviews with employees and so forth. Third, enforcement policies must be established. An example of monitoring international suppliers is Cadbury Schweppes. The company conducted detailed consultations with its supply chain partners and other associate or joint venture manufacturers. The aim was to ensure that consistently high standards of human rights and ethical trading are encouraged across all areas from which it derives raw materials. This commitment was underlined at Cadbury's Annual General Meeting (2001) when their chief executive announced that the company was reviewing its supply chain in Ghana following concerns about labour practices in the West African cocoa industry. Marks & Spencer (M&S) (one of the most successful retailers in the UK before it ran into trouble in 1998) was accused in January 1996 by a British TV channel, Granada, in its *World in Action* programme, of deliberately misleading its customers through labelling its St. Michael own-branded products with incorrect country-of-origin stickers. Moreover, it was alleged that M&S had used under-aged workers in the production process. M&S initiated a £1 million action plan by creating a 'hit squad' to audit its suppliers through randomly visiting foreign factories to ensure that they did not employ under-age workers. M&S also wrote to all its suppliers reminding them of the strict code of conduct and service obligations of being part of the M&S supply chain.

GREENING THE SUPPLY CHAIN

The topic of ethics and the environment has been discussed in Chapter 4, and therefore, this section focuses on issues related to the supply chain only.

Greening the supply chain management consists of the involvement of purchasing and supplying in activities that include reduction, recycling, reuse and the substitution of materials. It includes the examination of how intra and inter-organizational factors both drive and constrain suppliers' and purchasers' involvement in greening the supply chain activity. In simple terms, when a company imposes environmental conditions on the products and processes of its suppliers, it is called 'greening the supply chain'. As discussed in Chapter 4, companies cannot ignore environmental issues. Further, environmental standards should be met throughout the whole supply chain. The greening of the supply chain, however, poses several problems and challenges (Walton *et al.* 1998). Many companies have developed screening protocols for their suppliers that probe deeply into their internal management and engineering practices. Others have been more aggressive and have incorporated environmental criteria into their procurement specifications. For example, Hewlett Packard has developed a quantitative supplier rating system that takes into account their environmental improvement policies and implementation plans, as well as their elimination of ozone-depleting substances. The key challenge is how to make the vendors and sellers abide by the same internal ethical standards.

THE CASE OF NIKE

Nike has made environment performance a priority, reaching out beyond Nike-owned facilities to include manufacturing partners, suppliers and material vendors. In an effort to green its supply chain, in February 1993, the Nike Environmental Action Team (NEAT) arose out of Nike's efforts to coordinate specific environmental efforts around the world in the context of its business practices. NEAT's mission was to develop answers to the problems that Nike's business – and the sports industry as a whole – poses to the environment. Nike actively seeks partnership with ecologically responsible suppliers who have made a commitment to sound business practices. Facilities not meeting Nike's environmental business standards are offered assistance through NEAT representatives.

To help track its contractors' progress in reducing pollution, Nike supplies all chemical vendors, equipment suppliers and manufacturers with an educational programme which includes: an overview of Nike's objectives; its corporate environmental policy; a master substances list; legislation concerning products and packaging; executive summaries on all programmes so that factories/vendors know which programmes apply to them; a sustainability assessment; and labour practices programme information. In addition, Nike has developed a program for Management of Environmental Safety and Health (MESH) to help its manufacturing partners develop objectives and targets to reduce and eliminate environmental impacts.

Nike's objectives include its aim to:

- Integrate principles of sustainability into all major business decisions.
- Scrutinize its environmental impacts in its day-to-day operations and throughout every stage of the product life cycle.
- Design and develop product, materials and technologies according to the fundamental principles of sustainability.
- Promote Nike's practices throughout the supply chain and seek business partnerships with suppliers who operate in a manner consistent with Nike's values.
- Educate its employees, customers, and business partners to support its goal of achieving sustainability.
- Turn awareness into action by integrating environmental responsibility into job responsibility.

Nike's efforts have been emulated by many other leading firms operating in a wide range of different sectors. Ironically, despite evidence of good practice in the environmental area, Nike has had to contend with allegations that at least one key South East Asian subcontractor has made use of sweatshop labour.

SUMMARY

This chapter argues that the ethical challenges contained within the contemporary discourse of supply chain management should occasion no surprise. They mirror the challenges and contradictions facing other management functions, that is, the need of management to be able to be ethical but at the same time remain competitive, and the extent to which these be reconciled. However, given the fact that partners in the supply chain are often outside the reach of corporate governance, ethics in supply chain management poses an additional challenge. The conflictual element inherent in the relationship between firms and their suppliers needs to be recognized and dealt with. Firms should not, for instance, forbid their buyers from accepting gifts and gratuities that could influence their decisions, and reward their selling department for doing exactly the same. Further, firms should not wash their hands from any unethical actions by their suppliers and distributors. Given the changing relationship of suppliers and distributors, with more and more collaborations and information sharing, where suppliers and distributors are becoming partners in the production process, firms have to be responsible for the behaviour of their suppliers and distributors.

KEY QUESTIONS

1. Do you think the dominant firm in a supply chain should be responsible for the ethical conduct of its suppliers? Give reasons for your answer.
2. Introduce and critically discuss two ethical challenges facing today's supply chain manager.
3. Critically discuss General Motors' 'Policy Governing Gifts, Entertainment and Gratuities from Suppliers'. Do you think this policy does enough to ensure ethical conduct?
4. Can Nike's environmentally sound policies mean that the firm should be allowed greater leeway in its labour practices? Give reasons for your answer.

CASE STUDY: MONITORING THE SUPPLY CHAIN OF COCOA

Within supply chains, those at the end tend to be the most dominant. A major producer of chocolate, Cadbury Schweppes decided in early 2001 to review its entire supply chain in Ghana, a major producer of cocoa and Cadbury's major supplier (*Financial Times* 4/5/2001). This followed on concerns prompted by allegations of poor labour practices in the West African cocoa industry; the firm has traditionally avoided the Ivory Coast, where there is some evidence that child labour is employed (ibid.). Cadbury's will be working with the Corporate Citizenship Company (a consultancy firm specializing in ethical issues) to audit the relevant parts of its supply chain. Since the nineteenth century, Cadbury's has placed a strong premium on ethical conduct. Certainly, dominant users in a supply chain are in a powerful position to set the agenda.

ISSUES

Should the Cadbury's example be emulated by firms operating in other industries, and, if not, why not?

FURTHER READING

Emmelhainz, A.M. and Adams, J.R. 1999. 'The apparel industry response to sweat-shop concerns: a review and analysis of codes of conduct', *Journal of Supply Chain Management*, 35, 3: 51–7. This article reviews and analyses codes of the impact of conducts on sweatshops in the supply chain.

Cooper, R.W., Frank, G.L. and Kemp, R.A. 1997. 'The ethical environment facing the profession of purchasing and materials management', *International Journal of Purchasing and Materials Management*, 33, 2: 2–11. This article discusses the general ethical environment facing purchasing and material management professionals.

Turner, G.B., Taylor, G.S. and Hartley, M.F. 1994. 'Ethics policies and gratuity acceptance by purchasers', *International Journal of Purchasing and Material Management*, Summer, 30, 3. This article explores the issue of gratuity acceptance by purchasers.

ETHICS AND MARKETING

As is the case with the discipline of business ethics generally, there has been a proliferation of research on ethics in marketing. This literature is a particularly fragmented one. Nonetheless, a number of strands are apparent. These include debates surrounding the ethical duties (if any) of the marketing manager, the role of codes of ethics in marketing, and new forms of relationship between customer and client.

ADVERTISING AND ETHICS

Advertising constitutes the most visible form of marketing and today constitutes an essential component of trading (Harker and Harker 2000). Critics of contemporary advertising have suggested that it has become increasingly pervasive, intrusive and pernicious (Laczniak and Laczniak 1998). Whilst the origins of advertising can be traced back to the classical world, its different manifestations have greatly proliferated over the past 30 or so years. Indeed, advertising spending in the United States has expanded at a faster rate than the US economy as a whole (Laczniak and Laczniak 1998).

This has led postmodern writers such as Jean Baudrillard to suggest that our society has entered an age of what can be termed 'hyperreality'; differing forms of media have become so all pervasive – and increasingly realistic – that the gap between image and reality is not always easily distinguishable (Friedman 1992). Whilst the scale and extent of this process may be disputed, there is little doubt that modern forms of advertising have permeated the most remote corners of the earth. Collectively, marketing managers indeed have gained the power to shape the choices and lifestyles of the vast bulk of humanity. In turn, this creates a considerable range of responsibilities.

THE RELATIONSHIP BETWEEN MARKETING MANAGER AND THE CONSUMER

In *De Officiis*, the Roman philosopher, Cicero, argued that all vendors do have a range of moral duties towards their clients (Singhapakdi *et al.* 1999). However, what such duties are, and whether a particular set of duties is universal, is a somewhat contentious matter. Ferrell and Gresham argue that an individual's ethical framework is informed in a contingent fashion, reflecting the individual, social and cultural environments (quoted in Singhapakdi *et al.* 2000); what is deemed acceptable in one society may not be seen in another (Schlegelmilch 1998). For example, in an Islamic country in the third world, the aggressive marketing of alcohol would, to much of the population, be seen as an unethical act, but cigarette advertising – given the probability that less information may be commonly available on the hazards posed by smoking – less so. In contrast, in many Western countries, the converse would be the case.

However, this does not free marketing managers from having to take account of a bedrock of common ethical norms; in almost all societies, the aggressive marketing of both cigarettes and alcohol to vulnerable groupings such as the under-aged would be seen as an unethical act (Chonko 1995).

Nonetheless, in advertising – as in most other areas – there are considerable grey areas as to what constitutes ethical conduct. And, an ethical problem has to be perceived as an ethical problem for ethical decision making to take place (Singhapakdi *et al.* 1999). In practice, this means that marketing personnel have considerable leeway in deciding what constitutes ethical behaviour (Singhapakdi *et al.* 1999).

To neo-liberals, the act of marketing entails no ethical duties, other than those associated with the pursuit of profits. This would result in marketing being firmly embedded in what is assumed to be classic managerialism. The 'invisible hand' of the market will encourage firms to market in a suitable fashion – the products of firms that are touted in a distasteful or dishonest fashion to consumers will inevitably be eschewed. However, this approach is underpinned by the assumption of perfect knowledge (cf. Beauchamp and Bowie 1997). Consumers are not always aware of the particular hazards associated with a particular product, or may have uneven knowledge in this regard. Consumers in countries with higher overall levels of literacy and formal education are in a far stronger position to make an informed choice than their less well-off counterparts. Moreover, advertisements may be – and, indeed, often are – deliberately pitched at groupings that simply lack the capacity to make an informed choice at all, most notoriously the very young.

There is little doubt that a minimalist ethical approach has often contributed to the poor image of the marketer as a 'vendor of snake oil', a tout or con man (cf. Baumhart 1961). This in turn fuelled the rise of a consumerist movement, challenging the narrowly managerial view of marketing (Higgins 2000). There is little doubt that this forced the marketing agenda to alter to take on board the pressures of consumer lobbying; however, it can be argued that the good of the consumer can be reconciled with traditional marketing practice (Higgins 2000). For example, Kotler suggests that marketing can play a vital role in facilitating a mutual benefit exchange; 'active and diligent' consumers reward the firm that opens up new opportunities for enriching their life experience (Higgins 2000). Thus, marketing can be seen as a force for enlightenment.

However, this raises two questions, the first philosophical and the second practical. With regard to the former, adherents of the mainstream philosophical traditions (with the possible exception of the rights-based approach) would argue that marketing managers should still subject marketing to certain ethical tests. For example, for utilitarians advertising should make some contribution to overall happiness to be of some ethical worth; to virtue theorists, advertising should be grounded in a learned body of desirable values and behavioural constructs. Secondly, there is the practical dimension of monitoring and enforcement. There are many instances where firms have benefited from palpably unethical practices. It can be argued that it is vital that consumers are supplied with sufficient information to make informed choices, and that certain basic norms of behaviour (such as the protection of the most vulnerable in society) should be upheld.

Traditionally, there have been three approaches to customer service: manipulative, courteous and personalized (Buckley 2000). In other words, customers can simply be seen as persons to be duped, directed, and/or refocused in order that they may make certain purchases, as something of value to be treated with respect, or as one partner in what is hoped will be a long-term relationship. However, recent work has pointed to the dyadic nature of exchange – exchange relationships are, in many cases, not one-off affairs, whilst each party is likely to be influenced and shaped by the other (Buckley 2000; Singhapakdi *et al.* 1999). This means not only that, for the firm, the views of the customer are crucial, but also that both have certain ethical responsibilities. A number of studies have indicated that substantial ethics gaps tend to exist between marketer and potential customer, even although such gaps could be extremely counterproductive in ensuring that custom is retained (Singhapakdi *et al.* 1999).

Consumers are, of course, not always possessors of the necessary information to make an informed ethical choice. However, where there is widespread evidence – frequently aired in the popular media to the extent that it becomes common knowledge – to suggest that the consumption of certain products is unethical, then some responsibility must devolve on the consumer in a highly literate society, no matter how devious the vendor may have been. For example, there have been repeated exposes of the irreparable environmental damage caused by the unsustainable extraction of peat (for use in domestic gardens) and tropical hardwood. Nonetheless, in the UK, considerable consumer demand persists both for such peat, and for furniture constructed from tropical hardwood of unverifiable provenance. In short, the consumers have to make ethical decisions of their own (Singhapakdi *et al.* 1999). As with any other stakeholder grouping, it has been argued that consumers have a vital role to play in impelling firms towards more ethical conduct, and in monitoring compliance with basic ethical norms (see Chapter 2).

This does not, of course, excuse any ethical lapses by the vendor. It can be argued that whatever the relationship between buyer and seller, the ethical decision-making process of the marketer remains crucial (Singhapakdi *et al.* 1999). Whilst 'phoney smiles' may not constitute an ethical breach, there are many grey areas. For example, some writers, such as Ford, have charged that even the depersonalization of service in areas such as health care can constitute an ethical breach; the ability to rapidly gain the custom – and rapid turnover – of clients can easily be privileged over their long-term well-being (quoted in Buckley 2000).

A further issue is that of pricing. For example, it has often been argued that certain drugs are overpriced given that they are of vital need to sufferers; in practice, this means that the very poor may be denied treatment (Ferrell *et al.* 2000). Marketing is, of course, not only about the use of media, but also pricing policies. Particularly contentious has been the pricing of drugs to treat AIDS, and attempts by major drug companies to block the distribution of generic alternatives. It is often argued that high pricing funds future research. However, a large proportion of advances in medicine continue to be made in publicly funded laboratories and universities; critics have argued that taxpayers continue to subsidize corporate gain at the expense of the most vulnerable.

Finally, in marketing, ethical dilemmas not only concern the firm and potential consumers, but third parties as well. For example, a local authority or charity may accept donations in return for helping publicize a particular product or firm. Common examples would include those animal charities that display billboards advertising a particular brand of dog food on their premises, and/or include advertisements for such products in some of the media that they distribute. Such a relationship would be seen as mutually beneficial and unproblematic (provided, of course, that such food was of reasonable nutritional value).

More problematic was the decision by Guelph City Council (in the United States) to accept a donation from Imperial Tobacco Limited for the municipal theatre, naming the relevant facility after a well-known brand of cigarette in return (LeClair 1998). This decision sparked off a protracted public debate, although the local authority in question stuck by its decision. In short, in addition to the seller and potential buyer, any third party that is in a position to provide publicity to the marketer faces ethical dilemmas as well. Such third parties would not only include charities and other 'deserving causes', but also, of course, the mass media as well.

CODES OF ETHICS IN MARKETING

Many countries rely on self-regulation as a means of ensuring 'fair play' in advertising, backed up by codes of conduct. Whilst there is little doubt that certain forms of advertising can be misleading or harmful – an often-cited example are cigarette advertisements aimed at teenagers – self-regulation frees government charges of controlling the freedom of speech (Harker and Harker 2000; Laczniak and Laczniak 1985). However, the advertising industry – in most cases – has been unable to evade its responsibilities via self-regulation. Given the public nature of advertising, adherence to such codes of conduct tend to be closely monitored by government, social commentators and consumer groupings (Harker and Harker 2000). However, of course, the viability of self-regulation is heavily dependent on mutual co-operation and sufficient mechanisms to preclude free-riding rogue firms.

In other words, there have to be mechanisms in place to preclude a less scrupulous firm from deliberately breaking an advertising code in order to gain a short-term competitive advantage.

A further issue is the question as to who should have the responsibility of drafting codes of marketing ethics. On the one hand, it can be argued that a code drafted by outsiders can result in low levels of commitment by the affected firms (Harker and Harker 2000). On the other hand, a code of ethics that is unilaterally drafted by the affected industry is likely to lack legitimacy, and be ineffective. Consequently, should an industry have the responsibility of drafting its own code of ethics, wide-ranging consultation is necessary. Codes of ethics have tended to focus on areas such as the appropriateness of markets (e.g. restrictions against the promotion of cigarettes or alcohol to children). However, a basic degree of truthfulness, the degree to which comparisons are permitted, etc., there has been increasing political pressure for advertisements not to be overtly sexist or racist (Harker and Harker 2000); in practice the former generally tends to be seen as more acceptable than the latter.

ETHICAL MARKETING STRATEGIES: CAUSE-RELATED MARKETING

Cause-related marketing (CRM) incorporates a charitable dimension within an act of exchange. Here the vendor undertakes to give a specified amount to a designated charitable cause for each good or specific service purchased by the consumer. In some respects, CRM represents a manifestation of classic corporate philanthropy (Higgins 2000; Schlegelmilch 1991). However, CRM does incorporate a more strategic dimension – giving is deliberately targeted and closely linked to the performance of a particular product. The nature of sponsorship is thus firmly located within the realm of overall corporate activities. Higgins (2000) notes that CRM was sponsored by American Express in its 1981 promotion of the Fine Arts Group in California; since then the scope of American Express's charitable giving has greatly expanded. American Express's strategy has since been widely implemented. However, critics have charged that CRM may not be sustainable, and may have weakened other forms of fund raising, and, indeed, a tradition of free giving (Higgins 2000).

Nonetheless, there is little doubt that many charities have handsomely benefited from CRM. This has led a number of charities to take a proactive role in persuading firms to make use of CRM, a good example being the RSPCA and Kellogg's breakfast cereals (Higgins 2000). However, research has indicated that advertising agencies are likely to particularly focus their efforts on popular causes, such as illiteracy. More controversial – or uncomfortable – causes such as AIDS are widely shunned (Higgins 2000). In short, for CRM advertising campaigns to be successful, the sympathy must be gained of target audiences; above all, causes must be unthreatening (Higgins 2000).

A possible exception to this general rule would be the Benetton clothing advertising campaigns, which have focused on controversial issues such as AIDS, the death penalty, and clerical sexuality (Higgins 2000). Benetton advertisements have repetitively highlighted social taboos, including the depiction of dying people. Benetton advertising managers have argued that the advertisements represent a sincere attempt to open debates on key social issues 'of our time'. However, by their very nature, advertisements tend to be close-ended; they represent more of a (often sensationalist) one-off affair rather than the start of an informed debate. Indeed, to postmodern writers such as Baudrillard, such advertisements would simply represent a manifestation of a postmodern 'ecstatic age' – cheap sensation is privileged above substance (Friedman 1992). The amoral gaze is all that is offered, voyeurism rather than steps towards meaningful change (Higgins 2000).

There is little doubt that CRM is highly efficacious; surveys of consumers in the UK have revealed that 83 per cent of consumers have favourable images of brands associated with CRM (Higgins 2000). Whilst it is easy to dismiss CRM as a cynical marketing tool, research conducted by Teather has indicated that marketing managers engaging in CRM campaigns were partially motivated by sentiment; albeit that it was an effective marketing strategy, it resulted in, in the words of one marketing manager, 'a warm feeling inside' (quoted in Higgins 2000).

However, a deontologist would, in many respects, would be somewhat sceptical as to the moral worth of CRM (Higgins 2000). To adherents of this philosophical tradition, acts are only of moral worth if they were motivated for the right reasons; if CRM was adopted to increase sales of a particular product then it is of no moral significance. Any claims to ethical status would more easily be on utilitarian grounds; any act that enhances overall happiness is necessarily good.

Moreover, postmodernists would share the scepticism of deontologists. To Zygmunt Bauman, CRM quite simply removes moral behaviour from the hands of the 'other' (Higgins 2000; cf. Bauman 1993). In other words, charity giving is absolved by the act of exchange; rampant consumerism is given an acceptable moral face. In support of this assertion, Higgins (2000) cites the example of the American Express 'Charge Against Hunger' campaign. Through this campaign, alleviating the crisis of starvation was directly linked to consumerist acts such as the charging to a credit card of a meal in an expensive restaurant (Higgins 2000); alleviating privation could be reconciled with wanton plenty. Similarly, an Exxon advertising campaign linked donations to environmental causes with fuel consumption,

135

and, hence, indirectly, with the creation of pollution; existential discomforts could be reconciled with consumption (Higgins 2000). To Bauman (1993), this would reflect the relentless instrumentalization of society, and its reduction to the pursuit of image at the expense of real moral worth.

ETHICAL MARKETING STRATEGIES: GREEN MARKETING

The term 'green marketing' is often used interchangeably with 'sustainable' or 'environmental' marketing. Green marketing is an extremely loose concept. However, five broad approaches to green marketing can be identified; approaches which, however, are of very much broader relevance in providing a starting point for ethical marketing in the more general sense of the word. First, there is the 'fair play' approach; customers have a right to know what they are getting. This approach would be critical of attempts at 'greenwashing' (Crane 2000b). The latter refers to dubious environmental claims that are unverifiable (for example, claims that wood products have come from sustainable forestry operations, but with no independent corroboration), or patently false. 'Fair play' marketing would, for example, include clear labelling of cosmetic products that are not tested on animals (labelling certified by an independent monitoring organization), the absence of such a label implicitly denoting that such testing has indeed taken place. Consumers would thus be in a position to make an informed choice.

This has led writers such as Smith (2001) to propose a Consumer Sovereignty Test (CST) – does the target market know the risks and/or damages associated with a particular product? An example Smith highlights is the case of tobacco, a product that probably does not make a significant contribution to environmental degradation, but which poses a very real health hazard. The latter information is less common knowledge in many areas of the third world where tobacco is aggressively promoted (Smith 2001). Moreover, as noted elsewhere, tobacco is often marketed to teenagers, a grouping with 'reduced consumer capability'. Finally, tobacco being highly addictive reduces the capacity of even adult consumers who are fully conversant with the relevant health risks to make fully objective choices (Smith 2001). Similarly, given that all sentient beings have a capacity for suffering, consumers should be informed if a particular product was tested on animals (Smith 2001).

Secondly, there are approaches to green marketing that are simply 'managerialist'. Here, the consumer is seen as holding certain moral values, which the firm has to be seen to reconcile its activities with in order to gain market share (Crane 2000b). Ethical conduct is thus about placating the consumer, rather than necessitating a real change in corporate values.

Thirdly, there is the reformist approach. This approach suggests that the firm's activities have to be realigned with legitimate stakeholder expectations and needs; however, again, any reform in activities would partially be promoted by self-interest (Crane 2000b). In other words, the firm has to secure (and retain) a favourable image in the community, in order to keep (and expand) its market share.

Fourthly, there is the reconstructionist approach. This is founded in the 'deep green' frame of reference discussed in Chapter 4. Reconstructionists would argue that the marketer has to respond proactively to growing evidence of irreversible environmental degradation (Crane 2000b). Unregulated markets are, by their very nature, morally deficient; indeed, marketing is often part of the problem of environmental degradation, rather than part of the solution (Crane 2000b). However, it can be argued that business can play a central role in ensuring sustainable development; as the 'deep green' perspective has become mainstream, it has increasingly taken account of the role and potential of business in helping bring about a 'better world'. Nonetheless, a fundamental rethink in marketing strategy is in order (Crane 2000b).

'Deep green' marketing would adopt a minimalist approach in marketing products that were produced in a sustainable and human fashion, an often-cited example being the Body Shop range of cosmetics. However, this would only be one dimension of 'deep green' marketing; the latter should entail not just the promotion of specific products in a certain fashion, but also aim to change wider social values. By focusing on environmental issues, 'deep green' marketing can help raise consumer awareness of the major issues at stake. The 'deep green' marketing strategy does incorporate certain inherent contradictions. For example, would it ever be possible to market a motor car in a truly 'deep green' fashion? However, there is little doubt that many contemporary advertising campaigns do incorporate a 'deep green' dimension. Again, in the case of the motor industry (the above caveat notwithstanding), an example would be the Volkswagen advertising campaign that promoted the idea that motor cars should be fully recyclable and that consumers should take recyclability into account when choosing a vehicle.

Finally, the interpretavist perspective would focus on internal issues, and the extent to which morality can become embedded in the marketing sections of 'green organizations' (Crane 2000b). In other words, ethical issues should become part and parcel of the marketing process. Here William and Murphy suggest that virtue theories may provide a useful starting point: the question should be asked as to what kind of perceptions is the marketer seeking to mould, and what sort of organization should the virtuous individual wish to be associated with (Smith 2001). In other words, the extent to which 'green marketing' becomes an implicit assumption underlying any marketing decisions. This, perhaps, is the hardest approach to follow; however, again, environmental issues have become squarely mainstream. Many consumer products now incorporate clear environmental information either in advertisements and/or on the actual labelling of the product as a matter of course (for example, 'GM Free', 'Cruelty Free', 'Recyclable', 'Made from Recycled Plastic', etc.).

Whichever approach is followed, it is clear that firms have to take environmental issues increasingly seriously in advertising campaigns. Again, however, the question emerges as to whether this should be on the grounds of 'enlightened self-interest' or because it is the 'right' thing to do. Only the fourth and fifth of the above approaches would accord primacy to the latter, and as such, meet the deontological test of what constitutes ethical behaviour.

SUMMARY

Ethics represents a choice between different courses of action; conflict and disagreement is natural in choosing the 'best option' (Keyes 1997). Ethical theories provide useful guidelines for making decisions in marketing, but do not provide concrete solutions (Keyes 1997). There is little doubt that trust is an important driver of long-term exchange relationships; in marketing as in any other area, ethical conduct can be extremely good for business (Buckley 2000). However, there is more to ethical marketing than simply what is in the long term an interest of business. Important questions include the nature and extent of consumer knowledge and the capacity for the consumer to make an informed decision, the role of third parties, and the extent to which marketing practice should be ethically grounded even if there seems little prospect of financial reward for good practice.

KEY QUESTIONS

1. What ethical issues are likely to intrude into the relationship between marketing managers and their customers?
2. Is a code of ethics sufficient to ensure fair play in marketing? Give reasons for your answer.
3. Introduce and critically discuss the concept of 'green marketing'.

CASE STUDY: BECOMING RESPECTABLE – THE CASE OF PHILIP MORRIS

'Cigarettes kill people. Even the companies that make them now admit that. Indeed, Philip Morris, maker of the world's best-selling cigarette brand Marlboro, actually pointed out the 'benefits' of killing people last week.

It commissioned a study for the Czech Republic that concluded that its government saved £21m in 1999 through not having to support, house and care for smokers who died prematurely from tobacco-related illnesses.

In spite of the rather twisted moral logic of such an argument, the initiative was just the latest example of Philip Morris' new strategy of openness and "responsibility". Earlier this month it emerged that the company was working with London advertising agency Doner Cardwell Hawkins to develop a European campaign positioning it as more socially responsible.

Typically, a senior Philip Morris spokesman denies all knowledge of the campaign, although he admits that DCH has been "doing some development work for us".

The agency won't discuss the brief, but it is understood that the tobacco giant is trying to emulate the $100m-a-year campaign it has been running in the US that is trying to reposition Philip Morris for the 21st century. It concentrates on the range of public work and projects it funds using the endline: "Working to make a difference. The people of Philip Morris".

As part of its drive for respectability Philip Morris is also keen to position itself as the world's biggest packaged goods company, rather than a tobacco baron. Although two-thirds of Philip Morris' $80bn sales last year came from tobacco, its website makes great stock of the fact that its subsidiary Kraft is the world's second biggest food company and that it owns Miller, the second biggest brewer in the US.

Ironically, it seems it was this revelation that prompted pressure group Adbusters to place a powerful anti-Philip Morris ad in magazines such as *Harpers & Queen*. The ad pictures Kraft brands such as Maxwell House, Philadelphia and Shreddies, and the headline: "Why are you buying your food from a tobacco company?"

Philip Morris' new approach was crystallised in March when chairman and chief executive Geoffrey C. Bible launched a new mission statement to institutional investors: "To be the most responsible, effective and respected developer, manufacturer and marketer of consumer products, especially products intended for adults".

He said that only responsible manufacturers would have a role in shaping the industry's future and announced a strategy of "constructive engagement" with both government and pressure groups.

At the meeting, Bible even suggested that Philip Morris should work with the US government in regulating the tobacco industry, to which one shareholder quipped: "It's like the Ku Klux Klan helping develop civil rights laws".

But there is logic in this thinking. The holy grail for Philip Morris is to be seen as a credible business. It wants to validate tobacco – which is still a legal, taxed product – alongside other 'adult' drugs it makes, such as alcohol and coffee.

"We're seeking to be more responsive to society", says David Davies, vice-president for corporate affairs. "We will look at appropriate opportunities to communicate with societies generally about the values that we hold".' (*Financial Times* 24/7/2001).

ISSUES

Do you think that companies in controversial industries such as tobacco face advertising restrictions, even if they are not directly promoting their principal product, in this case, tobacco? Alternatively, does the sophisticated nature of Philip Morris's marketing strategies in the first world underscore the near impossibility of regulation in this area?

FURTHER READING

Baumhart, R. 1961. 'How ethical are businessmen?', *Harvard Business Review*, 38: 6–31. This article sets the scene for subsequent debates on marketing ethics.

Chonko, L. 1995. *Ethical Decision Making in Marketing*. Thousand Oaks: Sage. This book provides a relatively up-to-date perspective on some of the ethical challenges facing marketing managers.

Laczniak, P. and Laczniak, G. 1985. *Marketing Ethics: Guidelines for Managers*. Lexington: Lexington Books. Another valuable applied text on the problems, challenges and possibilities of ethical marketing.

 **ETHICAL BUSINESS: CHALLENGES AND THE WAY FORWARD**

There is little doubt that contemporary managers are faced with a vast range of ethical dilemmas. Inter alia, some of the most pressing questions fall into the four broad areas: relations with employees; relations with the community, environmental issues; and the consequences of globalization.

First, in an age of flexibility and downsizing, the psychological contract between employee and firm has been greatly weakened. Jobs are no longer for life; conversely, firms can no longer expect the same degree of loyalty from employees. Moreover, there has been an increasing divergence between managerial and employee pay; the latter has tended to stagnate, ostensibly to ensure greater competitiveness and to reduce inflation (but also reflecting the reduced bargaining power of employee collectives). In contrast, in many industries (ranging from transport to higher education), managerial pay has increased exponentially, ostensibly to secure the services of the most capable; in practice, however, the relationship between managerial pay and performance seems, in many cases, extremely tenuous or non-existent. This raises a fundamental question as to what remaining responsibilities managers have towards their the workforces: simply to ensure the continued survival of the firm, or to seek to fairly reward all members of the organization for effort expended? The latter may be for long-term reasons (the creation of a loyal, productive and committed workforce) and/or because of a perceived moral obligation managers may have to their subordinates.

Whatever one's views on the matter, it is clear that the 'social question' within the firm has returned to the agenda. Cavalier managers of semi-moribund firms who have increased their pay to the brink of looting are being increasingly 'named and shamed' in the media, even if formal mechanisms for holding them to account are very much weaker. The latter reflects both the product of over two decades of union decline (although there are signs of a limited recovery), and the reluctance of governments to take effective action, even in the case of organizations that heavily subsidized by the state.

Secondly, and related to the first, are relations between managers and communities. The concept of 'stakeholder' has gained increasing popularity. Even if managerial notions of accountability to the workforce have seemingly diminished since the early 1970s, there are increasing pressures to be accountable to a range of other players. More specifically, community organizations have proved highly effective in bringing firms to account; examples would include the role of Greenpeace in forcing Shell to review the scuttling of a redundant oil rig, and a coalition of organizations forcing Nike to review its labour practices in South East Asia.

The rise of broadly based community organizations – in part, a reflection of increased disillusionment with formal political processes – has resulted in a very real broadening of the discourse of management. Firms that fail to take account of the needs of key stakeholders – above all, the communities that will be most affected by their actions – face a range of pressures from adverse publicity to fully fledged consumer boycotts. However, it could be argued that firms also have a moral obligation to take account of those who have a direct or indirect interest in their activities. In other words, firms should take into account the interests of legitimate stakeholders irrespective of their capacity to make life difficult for management.

Thirdly, there is the question of the physical environment. The consequences of large-scale environmental degradation have become increasingly visible. These range from increasing global warming to the destruction of the ozone layer. There is a growing consensus around the need to take environmental issues more seriously, albeit that this has largely been prompted by health concerns. Moreover, the deep ecology view, once the preserve of radical environmentalists, has largely become mainstream. It is recognized that not just individual species need to be preserved or specific cases of environmental degradation are halted, but rather that entire ecosystems need to be conserved for both present and future generations. Moreover, there has been a growing recognition of the basic rights of all sentient beings: this has been reflected in increasing legal restrictions on animal experimentation and farming practices.

Whilst the conservative 'hard green' school, which sees the environment in terms of resources to be exploited for the primary benefit of humanity, remains influential – most notably in US governmental circles – even here this position has been modified, to take on board a broader range of concerns. There is little doubt that contemporary managers have to accord more attention to environmental issues than was the case a generation ago. This would reflect both consumer pressures and increased legislative strictures. However, whilst firms retain the option of regime shopping – and of relocating 'messy practices' to third world states, where both laws and civil society may be weaker – environmental issues have also permeated the core of ethical debates. Whilst environmental issues were in the past firmly subordinated to the need to ensure human progress, today conservation is seen as an inherent characteristic of sustainable development and growth.

Finally, there are the ethical dilemmas posed by globalization. As noted earlier in this volume, globalization is in fact an extremely loose term, but can be taken to encompass the integration of markets (and of consumer taste), rapid technological advance and interchange, and increasingly mobile financial capital. Firms are increasingly able to transfer operations between different national hosts, in search of laxer regulatory regimes, or simply cheaper labour. It can be argued that a little development is better than none, and that poor regions may benefit from such a process. However, in practice, it may exact unacceptable social costs, both to 'loser' regions and states who face capital flight and, ultimately, to 'beneficiary' communities if the price is the wanton destruction of natural resources and massive social dislocation. Moreover, whilst free trade may open up new opportunities, it may also result in distorted pricing, entrenching the dominance of end users in global commodity chains, with producers of raw materials only receiving a tiny percentage of end value. Again, these developments have led to a broadening of the ethical discourse: issues including fair trade (more specifically, 'fair' prices for primary commodities) and global labour standards have increasingly become mainstream. Firms, however, retain the choice of becoming proactive in this area, or simply adjusting their behaviour when impelled to by consumer pressure and/or legislation in their 'home nation'.

The ethical dilemmas facing the transnational corporations are particularly pronounced. As noted earlier, there is often considerable variation in laws and enforcement between provinces, states, regions and continents. Moreover, transnationals are faced with the task of transferring what are often socially specific moral norms into a global context. However, as Singer (1995) notes, ethics are universal. For example, to utilitarians, there is a set of behaviour that will, within a specific social context, increase overall happiness or diminish it; for deontologists, there is a set of behaviour that is objectively desirable and whose outcomes we would like to be at the receiving end of. Whilst the choice of philosophical tools may differ, managers of transnationals cannot escape ethical questions as easily as they may escape specific regulatory regimes; in a globalizing world, consumer pressure and the compass of transnational institutions, cuts across national boundaries.

To the bulk of philosophical perspectives on ethics, 'good' behaviour matters; it is, quite simply, desirable to do the 'right' thing. Even the seemingly amoral postmodern tradition, with its emphasis on the multi-facetted power struggles that wrack organizations and society, accords specific attention to the potentially undesirable consequences of domination and subordination. Whilst an argument may be made for moral relativism – what is desirable for one society may be undesirable for another – it can be argued that some actions are ethical and others are not regardless of social context. In other words, some actions may result in the worsening of the human condition – and indeed, that of the entire biosphere – and some a bettering. Whilst the consequences of specific actions may be both seen and unforeseen, this does not absolve actors from the need to consider ethical issues. With the possible exception of the radical rights-based approach, with its belief that individual rights are paramount and that regulation should be as minimal as possible in order that these may not be jeopardized, it is evident that philosophers are united in their belief that upholding ethical behaviour is a worthwhile end in itself. Indeed, ethical conduct should be seen as distinct from any other goals, such as the pursuit of profits.

This brings us to the question of unintended consequences. If an action has a positive outcome but was prompted by other motives – such as consumer pressures – is it ethical at all? This question is a particularly pressing one in the advanced societies. Firms are under increasing pressure to be seen to act ethically in a range of areas, from the environmental policies to marketing practices. To utilitarians, all actions that produce desirable outcomes (an increase in overall happiness) are ethical; there is little point in dissecting the rationale of key players. To deontologists and virtue theorists actions are only ethical if they are prompted for the right reasons. In other words, by focusing only on outcomes, utilitarians free managers and others from firmly grounding their behaviour on a moral foundation (be the latter the product of rules or simply cultivated virtues). To the authors, there is no little merit in both these perspectives. However, we do believe that increasing external pressures on firms to be seen to act ethically should not absolve managers from the responsibility to take ethical issues seriously for their own sake. In other words, managers should seek to infuse an ethical dimension into their actions, even in areas where popular scrutiny or market pressure may be slight. Decision making should encompass an ethical dimension, even if it is simply an ad-hoc utilitarian costs-benefits analysis, but with both these variables being seen in financial *and* 'overall condition' terms.

But, if managers *should* act ethically, must they, under certain circumstances, be compelled to? The authors believe that, under certain circumstances, ethics are too serious a business to be left purely to managers. We share with Adam Smith a belief in the importance of cooperation and trust, and the indispensability of a basic degree of social solidarity, a belief Smith expounds at great length in his *Theory of Moral Sentiments*, but also touches on in *The Wealth of Nations*.

It has been argued that the distinction between unethical and ethical behaviour may be simply one between short and long termism. In other words, by acting ethically, firms are securing their long-term survival, wisely husbanding both their resources and those of the external environment to which they have access. In contrast, the 'unethical' short termist will engage in behaviour that constitutes little more than 'slash and burn capitalism'. The latter would be characterized by future livings being jeopardized by the wanton destruction of natural resources, and/or with present activities being both a source of potential wealth to a few, but also the source of misery to many in surrounding communities. Businesspeople simply have the choice of being 'rude and ignorant farmers' relentlessly squandering resources and goodwill to their ultimate ruin or 'skilled and scientific farmers' who act in such a manner as to ensure their own survival and the prosperity of the community at large (cf. Hobson 1902).

Whilst it could be argued that 'good farmers' will ultimately drive out 'bad', this discounts the perennial free-rider problem. In unrestrained free markets, firms can often seize a short-term advantage by acting unscrupulously. For example, the global dominance of Far Eastern textiles manufactures was partially built on extremely repressive labour policies and uncontrolled pollution. The same could be said for many 'respectable firms' operating in the West, if their activities a century ago are considered. However, the argument that 'robber barons' will ultimately seek respectability – that firms will inevitably clean up their acts, once their dominance has been secured, in order to promote stability within their sphere of operations – does not always hold water. Entire industries continue to be characterized by unethical practices, 'bad' firms often do drive out 'good' ones, whilst the elimination of excesses in the mature societies has often directly contributed to their reappearance on the periphery.

It can be further argued that the unethical/short-term–ethical/long-term distinction is unnecessarily crude. We have seen that unethical behaviour can, in some instances, pay certainly over the medium, and, possibly, the long terms. Conversely, firms may seize a short-term advantage over competitors as a result of favourable publicity engendered by ethical behaviour. Even in a phase of aggressive growth, firms may benefit from being seen to be acting ethically, an example being the rise of the Body Shop chain of cosmetic stores in the UK. Moreover, an emphasis on the long term does not absolve managers from very real ethical responsibilities.

What, then is to be done? To the authors, institutions matter. The effects of particular financial, political, cultural and economic institutions are, as Richard Whitley (1999: 54) argues, particularly visible when the strength of a particular feature is either very high or low. The institutional context is reflected not only in formal laws and regulations, but also in unwritten rules and norms governing human behaviour. What managers do is partially framed by both the formal and latter. Laws designed to ensure ethical behaviour – be their strictures against pollution or minimum labour standards – can strengthen the hand of the ethical vis-à-vis the free-rider. They can also – by, say, linking good practice with access to markets – reward good conduct and penalize bad.

Above all, laws can help promote greater social solidarity, which is one of the major outcomes of ethical behaviour on a sustained and comprehensive basis. A bedrock of ethical theory is a belief in the necessity of ensuring that one's actions are not solely aimed at one's exclusive benefit; even radical neo-liberals locate the pursuit of profit in terms of the need to promote general wealth. Social solidarity does not only result in reduced levels of disruptive conflict, but can also make the world a safer one in which to do business. Firms can count on a minimum degree of 'good practice' from their partners and clients, which will help make a rapidly changing context more predictable, and facilitate long-term planning. Indeed, it can be argued that commitment to a firm is thus partially about commitment to the community at large.

However, managers can, through ethical conduct, help perpetuate the unwritten rules and strictures that underpin an institutional context. Ethics can be partially secured by laws, but also must be borne out through actions; institutions are partially reconstituted through human deeds (Giddens 1984). In other words, whilst the wider institutional context may shape the actions of individuals and collectives, these institutions in turn are continuously reconstituted through human actions (Giddens 1984). Through a relentless search for loopholes – or simply by relocating – individuals and firms can undermine the most stringent legislation. Whilst laws may 'help' managers on an ethical path, ethics are ultimately about decisions and actions, about the effects of very human choices. We would argue that whilst ethical conduct may often be financially lucrative, managers have to take ethics seriously, not only to secure long-term profitability but also to help reconstitute an institutional context that underpins the very existence of the firm.

SUMMARY

In today's world, with a strong emphasis on flexibility and downsizing, the psychological contract between employer and employee has been weakened. This raises the question as to what commitments and obligations remain between employers and employees. It can be argued that rather than a short-term focus on the pursuit of profitability, managers should consider both the long-term relationship between the firm and its workforce, and understand that the need to ensure corporate survival does not absolve managers from very real moral choices. Moreover, the relationship between managers and communities deserves serious consideration; firms can no longer ignore the interests of the wider community for both ethical and practical reasons. Again, with growing visible evidence of long-term environmental damages, green issues can no longer be deferred 'until the next generation'. The forces of globalization and the increasing power of TNCs again pose a specific set of pressing ethical dilemmas. However, the authors believe that ethical conduct should not be justified solely on the grounds of long-term economic rationality (as adverse to the relentless accumulation of profits on a short-term basis): managers have broader obligations to themselves and to wider society to take ethics seriously.

BIBLIOGRAPHY

Alexander, M. 2000. 'Economy reaps benefits from recycling', *Waste Age*, 31, 11: 24–5.

American Management Association website (www.amanet.org/usindex.htm).

Anderson, G.D. 1985. 'A fresh look at standards of professional conduct', *Journal of Accounting*, 160, 3: 91–106.

Anderson, G.D. and Ellyson, R.C. 1986. 'Restructuring professional standards: the Anderson reports', *Journal of Accountancy*, 160, 3: 92–104.

Anderson, J.C. and Narus, J.A. 1990. 'A model of distributor firm and manufacturer firm working partnerships', *Journal of Marketing*, 54: 42–58.

Andrews, C. 2000. 'Better environmental decisions: strategies for governments, business and communities', *Journal of the American Planning Association*, 66, 4: 453–4.

Anonymous. 1999. 'Manufacturers go green', *Professional Safety*, 44, 8: 35–7.

Anonymous. 2000. 'Environmental work is a good investment', *ENR*, 245, 1: 74–8.

Apeldoorn, B. 2000. 'Transnational class agency and European governance: the case of the European round table of industrialists', *New Political Economy*, 5, 2: 157–81.

Arestis, P. and Marshall, M. 1995. 'Obstacles to and strategies for the achievement of full employment', in Arestis, P. and Marshall, M. (eds), *The Political Economy of Full Employment: Conservatism, Corporatism and Institutional Change*. Aldershot: Edward Elgar.

Argenti, J. 1976. *Corporate Collapse: The Causes and Symptoms*. London: McGraw-Hill.

Aristotle. 1952. *Politics*. London: Everyman.

Arvey, R.D. and Sackett, P.R. 1993. 'Fairness in selection: current developments and perspectives', in Schmitt, N. and Borman, W. (eds), *Personnel Selection*. San Francisco: Jossey-Bass.

Ashkenas, R.N. 1990. 'A new paradigm for customer and supplier relationships', *Human Resources Management*, 29, 4: 385–96.

Attfield, R. 1999. *The Ethics of the Global Environment*. Edinburgh: Edinburgh University Press.

Austin, J. 1998 'Business leadership lessons from the Cleveland turnaround', *California Management Review*, 41, 1: 86–106.

Baird, L. and Meshoulam, I. 1988. 'Managing the two fits of strategic human resource management', *Academy of Management Review*, 13, 1: 116–28.

Baker, B. and Cooper, J. 1996. Occupational Testing Practice: Why might theory and practice contradict? Paper delivered to the First Conference on Ethical Issues in

Contemporary Human Resource Management, Imperial College Management School, London, 3 April.

Baker, B. and Cooper, J. 2000. 'Occupational testing and psychometric instruments: an ethical perspective', in Winstanley, D. and Woodall, J. (eds), *Ethical Issues in Contemporary Human Resource Managemant*. London: Macmillan, pp. 59–84.

Bansal, P. and Roth, K. 2000. 'Why companies go green', *Academy of Management Journal*, 43, 4: 717–36.

Barath, R. and Hugstad, P.S. 1977. 'Professionalism and the behavior of procurement managers', *Industrial Marketing Management*, 6: 297–306.

Barmash, I. 1973. *Great Business Disasters*. New York: Ballantine Books.

Barry, E.C. 1999. 'Economic analysis of accountants' ethical standards: the case of audit opinion shopping', *Journal of Accounting and Public Policy*, 18, 4/5: 339–63.

Bateman, T.B. and Zeithaml, C. 1989. 'The psychological context of strategic decisions'. *Strategic Management Journal*, 10: 587–92.

Bauman, Z. 1993. *Postmodern Ethics*. Oxford: Blackwell.

Baumhart, R. 1961. 'How ethical are businessmen?', *Harvard Business Review*, 38: 6–31.

Beardwell, I. and Holden, L. 1997. *Human Resource Management: A Contemporary Perspective*. London: Pitman.

Beardwell, I. and Holden, L. 2001. *Human Resource Management: A Contemporary Approach*. London: Prentice Hall.

Beauchamp, T. and Bowie, N. 1997. 'Ethical theory and business practice', in Beauchamp, T. and Bowie, N. (eds), *Ethical Theory and Business*. Upper Saddle River, NJ: Prentice Hall.

Beckman, J.K., Byington, J.R. and Munter, P.H. 1989. 'Regulating financial reporting: the debate continues', *Business*, 39, 1: 56–60.

Beer, M., Spector, B., Laurance, P., Mills, Q. and Walton, R. 1984. *Managing Human Assets*. New York: Free Press.

Behn, R.D. 1977. *Policy Termination: A Survey of the Current Literature and an Agenda for Future Research*. Washington, DC: Ford Foundation.

Bellman, K. and Khare, A. 2000. 'Economic issues in recycling end-of-life vehicles', *Technovation*, 20, 12: 677–90.

Berstein, A. 1997. 'Analysis and commentary: business backs an initiative on global working conditions', *Business Week*, October 20, p. 39.

Blustein, P. 1997. 'Apparel industry reaches agreement to end sweatshops in U.S. and abroad', *The Washington Post*, April 10, p. A19.

Bowie, N. 1991. 'Business ethics as a discipline: the search for legitimacy', in Freeman, R. (ed.), *Business Ethics: The State of the Art*. Oxford: Oxford University Press.

Bowie, N. 1997. 'New directions in corporate social responsibility', in Beauchamp, T. and Bowie, N. (eds), *Ethical Theory and Business*. Upper Saddle River, NJ: Prentice Hall.

Breitenfellner, A. 1997. 'Global unionism: a potential player', *International Labour Review*, 136, 4: 531–55.

Brenkert, G.G. 1981. 'Privacy, polygraphs and work', *Business and Professional Ethics Journal*, 1, 1: 19–35.

Brennan, A. 1993. 'Environmental decision making', in Berry, R.J. (ed.), *Environmental Dilemmas: Ethics and Decisions*. London: Chapman and Hall.

Brenner, S.N. and Cochran, P.L. 1991. 'The stakeholder theory of the firm: implications for business and society theory and research', *International Association for Business and Society Proceedings*: 449–67.

Breton, G. and Taffler, R.J. 1995. 'Creative accounting and investment analyst response', *Accounting and Business Research*, 25, 98: 81–93.

Brown, R.D. 1994. 'Corporate governance: the director as watchdog, juggler or fall guy', *Canadian Business Review*, 21, 1: 39–45.

Browne, M. and Kubasek, N. 1999. 'A communitarian green space between market and political rhetoric about environment law', *American Business Law Journal*, 37, 1: 127–69.

Buckics, R.M.L. 1999. 'Exploring ethical decisions', *The Internal Auditor*, 56, 5: 19–20.

Buckley, N. 2000. 'Review: communicating with customers', *Journal of the Academy of Marketing Science*, 28, 2: 312–13.

Buller, P., Kohls, J. and Anderson, K. 1997. 'A model for addressing cross-cultural ethical conflicts', *Business and Society*, 36, 2: 169–93.

Burns, R. 2000a. 'Enlightenment', in Burns, R. and Raymond-Pickard, H. (eds), *Philosophies of History*. Oxford: Blackwell.

Burns, R. 2000b. 'On philosophising history', in Burns, R. and Raymond-Pickard, H. (eds), *Philosophies of History*. Oxford: Blackwell.

Bylinsky, G. 1991. 'How companies spy on employees', *Fortune*, 4 November: 131–40.

Cameron, K.S., Sutton, R. and Whetten, D. (eds) 1998. *Readings in Organizational Decline: Frameworks, Research, and Prescriptions*. Cambridge, MA: Ballinger.

Carroll, A. 1979. 'A three-dimensional conceptual model of corporate social performance', *Academy of Management Review*, 4: 497–505.

Caroll, A. 1993. *Business and Society: Ethics and Stakeholders Management*. Cincinnati: South-Western Publishing.

Carter, C. 2000. 'Precursors of unethical behavior in global supplier management,' *Journal of Supply Chain Management*, 36, 1: 45–56.

Casey, B. and Gold, M. 2000. *Social Partnerships and Economic Performance*. Cheltenham: Edward Elgar.

Chang, S.J. and Ha, D. 2001. 'Corporate governance in the twenty-first century: new managerial concepts for supernational corporations', *American Business Review*, 19, 2: 32–44.

Chonko, L. 1995. *Ethical Decision Making in Marketing*. Thousand Oaks: Sage.

Clarkson Centre for Business Ethics. 2000. *Principles of Stakeholder Management*. Toronto: CCBE.

Clarkson, M.B.E. 1988. 'Corporate social performance in Canada, 1976–86', in Preston, L.E. (ed.), *Research in Corporate Social Performance and Policy, Vol. 10*: 241–65. Greenwich, CT: JAI Press.

Clarkson, M.B.E. 1991. 'The moral dimension of corporate social iesponsibility', in Coughlin, R.M. (ed.), *Morality, Rationality, and Efficiency: New Perspectives on Socio-Economics*. New York: M.E. Sharpe.

Clarkson, M.B.E. 1995. 'A stakeholder framework for analyzing and evaluating corporate social performance', *Academy of Management Review*, 20: 92–117.

Cohen, S. 1995. 'Stakeholders and consent', *Business and Professional Ethics*, 14, 1: 3–16.

Cooper, D. and Robertson, I. 1995. *The Psychology of Personnel Selection*. London: Routledge.

Cooper, R.W., Frank, G.L. and Kemp, R.A. 1997. 'The ethical environment facing the profession of purchasing and materials management', *International Journal of Purchasing and Materials Management*, 33, 2: 2–11.

Corveers, F. and van Veen, T. 1995. 'On the measurement of corporatism', *Labour*, 9, 3: 423–42.

Cottell, P.G. Jr., and Perlin, M.T. 1990. *Accounting Ethics: A Practical Guide for Professionals*. Westport, CT: Quorum Books.

Crane, A. 2000a. 'Corporate greening as amoralization', *Organizational Studies*, 21, 4: 673–96.

Crane, A. 2000b. 'Marketing and the natural environment', *Journal of Marketing*, 20, 2: 144–54.

Crouch, C. 1993. *Industrial Relations and European State Traditions*. Oxford: Clarendon.

Cummings, G.E. 1979. 'Are purchasing ethics being put to the test?', *Iron Age*, 222: 21–4.

Currie, E. and Skolnick, J. 1988. *America's Problems: Social Issues and Public Policy*. Glenview: Scott, Foresman and Company.

Cyert, R.M. 1978. 'The management of universities of constant or decreasing size', *Public Administration Review*, 38: 344–9.

Danely, J., Harrick, E., Strickland, D. and Sullivan, G. 1991. 'HR ethical situation', *Human Resource Management*, 26 June: 1–12.

D'Aveni, R.A. 1989. 'Dependability and organizational bankruptcy: an application of agency and prospect theory', *Management Science*, 35: 1120–38.

D'Aveni, R.A. 1990. 'Top managerial prestige and organizational bankruptcy', *Organization Science*, 21: 142.

De Castro, J.O., Meyer, G.D., Strong, K.C. and Uhlenbruck, N. 1996. 'Government objectives and organisational characteristics: a stakeholder view of privatisation effectiveness', *International Journal of Organisational Analysis*, 4, 4: 373–92.

De George, T.R. 1986. *Business Ethics*. London: Macmillan.

Delener, N. 1998. 'An ethical and legal synthesis of dumping', *Journal of Business Ethics*, 17, 15: 1747–53.

Deleuze, G. and Guattari, F. 1988. *A Thousand Plateaus*. Minneapolis: University of Minnesota Press.

Diller, J. 1999. 'A social conscience of the global marketplace', *International Labour Review*, 138, 2: 99–129.

Dobler, D.W. and Burt, D.N. 1996. *Purchasing and Supply Management*. New York: McGraw-Hill.

Dobson, J. 1992. 'Ethics in the transnational corporation: the "moral buck" street', *Journal of Business Ethics*, 11, 1: 21–43.

Dobson, J. 1997. *Finance Ethics: The Rationality of Virtue*. Oxford: Rowman and Littlefield.

Donaldson, T. 1991. 'Rights in the global market', in Freeman, R. (ed.), *Business Ethics: The State of the Art*. Oxford: Oxford University Press.

Donaldson, T. 1999. 'Making stakeholder theory whole', *Academy of Management Review*, 24: 237–41.

Donaldson, T. and Preston, L.E. 1995. 'The stakeholder theory of the corporation: concepts, evidence and implications', *Academy of Management Review*, 20: 65–91.

Driscoll, D. and Hoffman, M. 1998. 'HR plays a central role in ethics programs', *Workforce*, April edition.

Drummond, J. and Bain, B. 1994. *Managing Business Ethics: Management Reader.* Oxford: Butterworth Heinemann.

Emmelhainz, A.M. and Adams, J.R. 1999. 'The apparel industry response to sweatshop concerns: a review and analysis of codes of conduct', *Journal of Supply Chain Management*, 35, 3: 51–7.

Environmental Management Systems. 'Environmental Management Systems Home Page'. Raleigh: North Carolina Division of Pollution Prevention and Environmental Assistance (www.p2pays.org).

Evan, W. and Freeman, R. 1988. 'A stakeholder theory for the modern corporation: Kantian capitalism', in Beauchamp, T. and Bowie, N. (eds), *Ethical Theory and Business.* Englewood Cliffs: Prentice Hall.

Evensky, J. 2001. 'Adam Smith's lost legacy', *Southern Economic Journal*, 67, 3: 497–517.

Fedders, J.M. and Perry, L.G. 1984. 'Policing financial disclosure fraud: the SEC's top priority', *Journal of Accountancy*, 158, 1: 58–64.

Felo, A. 2001. 'Ethics programs, board involvement, and potential conflicts of interest in corporate governance, *Journal of Business Ethics*, 32, 3: 205–18.

Ferrel, O.C. and Gresham, L.G., 1985. 'A contingency framework for understanding ethical decision-making in marketing', *Journal of Marketing*, 49: 87–96.

Ferrell, O.C., Fraedrich, J. and Ferrell, L. 2000. *Business Ethics: Ethical Decision Making and Cases.* Boston: Houghton-Miffen.

Finn, D., Chonko, L. and Hunt, S. 1988. 'Ethical problems in public accounting: the view from the top', *Journal of Business Ethics*, 7: 605–15.

Finn, D.W., Munter, P. and McCaslin, T.E. (1994). 'Ethical perceptions of CPAs', *Managerial Auditing Journal*, 9, 1: 23–8.

Flanagan, R. 1999. 'Macro-economic performance and collective bargaining: an international perspective', *Journal of Economic Literature*, 37: 1150–75.

Frederick, W. 1991. 'The moral authority of transnational corporate codes', *Journal of Business Ethics*, 10, 3: 165–78.

Freeman, R.E. 1984. *Strategic Management: A Stakeholder Approach.* Boston: Pitman.

Freeman, R.E. 1991. 'Business ethics as an academic discipline', in Freeman, R. (ed.), *Business Ethics: The State of the Art.* Oxford: Oxford University Press.

Freeman, R.E. and Gilbert, D., Jr. 1988. *Corporate Strategy and the Search for Ethics.* Englewood Cliffs, NJ: Prentice Hall.

Friedman, J. 1992. 'Narcissism, roots, and postmodernity', in Lash, S. and Friedman, J. (eds), *Modernity and Identity.* Oxford: Blackwell.

Friedman, M. 1970. 'The social responsibility of business is to increase its profits', *New York Times Magazine*, 122, 126: 32–3, 122, 126.

Friedman, M. 1997. 'The social responsibility of business is to increase its profits', in Beauchamp, T. and Bowie, N. (eds), *Ethical Theory and Business.* Upper Saddle River, NJ: Prentice Hall.

Frooman, J. 1999. 'Stakeholder influence strategies', *Academy of Management Review*, 24: 191–205.

Fussell, L. and George, S. 2000. 'The institutionalization of environmental concerns', *International Studies of Management and Organization*, 30, 3: 41–58.

Gandtz, J. and Hayes, N. 1988. 'Teaching business ethics', *Journal of Business Ethics*, 7: 657–69.

Gebert, D. and Boerner, S. 1999. 'The open and closed corporation as distinctive forms of organization', *Journal of Applied Behavioral Science*, 35, 3: 341–59.

Gibson, K. 2000. 'The moral basis of stakeholder theory', *Journal of Business Ethics*, 26, 3: 245–57.

Giddens, A. 1984. *The Constitution of Society*. Cambridge: Polity.

Gilbert, R. 1991. 'Respect for persons, management theory and business ethics', Freeman, R. (ed.), *Business Ethics: The State of the Art*. Oxford: Oxford University Press.

Goldstein, M. and Madtes, C. 2000. 'The state of garbage in America', *BioCycle*, 41, 11: 40–8.

Goodpaster, K. 1991. 'Business ethics and stakeholder analysis', *Business Ethics Quarterly*, 1: 53–73.

Goodstein, J., Gautam, K. and Boeker, W. 1994. 'The effects of board size and diversity on strategic change', *Strategic Management Journal*, 15: 241–50.

Graber, D.E. 1979. 'Ethics enforcement – how effective?', *The CPA Journal*, 49, 9: 11–17.

Graybill, A. 2000. 'Losing paradise: the growing threat to our animals, our environment, and ourselves', *Library Journal*, 125, 14: 244–6.

Green, K., Morton, B. and New, S. 2000. 'Greening organisations', *Organization & Environment*, 13, 2: 206–25.

Griffiths, I. 1986. *Creative Accounting*. London: Sidgwick.

Guest, D. 1987. 'Human resource management and industrial relations', *Journal of Management Studies*, 24, 5: 503–21.

Guest, D. 2001. 'Industrial relations and human resource management', in Storey, J. (ed.), *Human Resource Management*. London: Thomson Learning.

Hakim, C. 1990. 'Core and periphery in employers' workforce strategy: evidence from the 1987 ELUS survey', *Work, Employment and Society*, 4: 157–88.

Hannan, M.T. and Freeman, J. 1984. 'Structural inertia and organizational change,' *American Sociological Review*, 49: 75–94.

Harker, D. and Harker, M. 2000. 'The role of codes of conduct in the advertising self-regulatory framework', *Journal of Macromarketing*, 20, 2: 155–66.

Harris, J.F. and McKay, P. 1997. 'Companies agree to meet on sweatshops', *The Washington Post*, August 3, p. A10.

Harrison, R. 1993. 'Case study: farm animals', Berry, R.J. (ed.), *Environmental Dilemmas: Ethics and Decisions*. London: Chapman and Hall.

Hartman, L.P. 1988. 'The rights and wrongs of workplace snooping', *Journal of Business Strategy*, 19, 3: 16–20.

Hau L.L. and Billington, C. 1995. 'The evolution of supply-chain-management models and practice at Hewlett-Packard', *Interfaces*, September–October, 25: 42–63.

Heery, E. 2000. 'The new pay: risk and representation at work', in Winstanley, D. and Woodall, J. (eds), *Ethical Issues in Contemporary Human Resource Management*. London: Macmillan.

Heide, J.B. and John, G. 1990. 'Alliances in industrial purchasing: the determinants of joint action in buyer–supplier relationships', *Journal of Marketing Research*, 27: 24–36.

Higgins, M. 2000. 'Cause-related marketing', *Business and Society*, 39, 3: 304–22.

Hobson, J. 1902. *Imperialism: A Study*. London: Allen and Unwin.

Hoffman, W. 1997. 'Business and environmental ethics', Beauchamp, T. and Bowie, N. (eds), *Ethical Theory and Business*. Upper Saddle River, NJ: Prentice Hall.

Hoffman, W. and Moore, J. Mills. 1990. *Business Ethics: Readings and Cases in Corporate Morality*. New York: McGraw-Hill.

Hofstede, G. 1980. *Cultures Consequences: International Differences in Work-Related Values*. Beverly Hills, CA and London: Sage.

Hosmer, L. 1987. 'Ethical analysis and human resource management', *Human Resource Management*, 26: 313–30.

Howard, M. 1996. 'Downsizing to destruction', *Management Accounting*, 74, 7: 66–70.

HR Magazine. 1999. 'Turn employees into saints?', *HR Magazine*, 44, 13.

Huselid, M. 1995. 'The impact of human resource management practices on turnover, productivity and corporate financial performance', *Academy of Management Journal*, 38, 3: 635–72.

Huxham, C. and Vangen, S. 2000. 'Ambiguity, complexity and dynamics in the membership of collaboration', *Human Relations*, 53, 6: 771.

Hyman, R. 1997. 'Trade unions and European integration', *Work and Occupations*, 24, 3: 309–31.

Iankova, E. 1996. 'Labour relations and political change in Eastern Europe', *Industrial and Labor Relations Review*, 50, 1: 177–86.

Iles P. and Robertson, I. 1997. 'Impact of selection procedures', in Anderson, N. and Herriot, P. (eds), *International Handbook of Assessment and Selection*. Chichester: Wiley.

IPD. 1997. *The IPD Code of Professional Conduct and Disciplinary Procedures*. London: Institute of Personnel and Development.

Jackson, D. 2001. 'Hard green: saving the environment from the environmentalists', *Forest Products Journal*, 51, 1: 7–14.

Jackson, K. 1997. 'Globalizing corporate ethics programmes', *Journal of Business Ethics*, 16, 12/13: 1227–35.

Jackson, K. 1998. 'A transnational court for transnational corporate wrongdoing: why the time is right', *Journal of Business Ethics*, 17, 7: 738–57.

Jackson, P. 1997. 'Downsizing and selection', in Anderson, N. and Herriot, P. (eds), *International Handbook of Assessment and Selection*. Chichester: Wiley.

Jameson, M. 1988. *Practical Guide to Creative Accounting*. London: Kogan Page.

Janyashankar, M.S., Smith, S.F. and Sadeh, N.M. 1996. *A Multi Agent Framework for Modeling Supply Chain Dynamics*. Technical Report, The Robotics Institute, Carnegie Mellon University.

Jawahar, I. and McLaughlin, G. 2001. 'Toward a descriptive stakeholder theory: an organizational life cycle approach', *Academy of Management. The Academy of Management Review*, 26: 397–414.

Jones, T.M. 1995. 'Instrumental stakeholder theory: a synthesis of ethics and economics', *Academy of Management Review*, 20: 404–37.

Jones, T.M. and Wicks, A.C. 1999. 'Convergent stakeholder theory', *Academy of Management Review*, 24: 206–21.

Kant, I. 2000. 'Progress in history', in Burns, R. and Raymond-Pickard, H. (eds), *Philosophies of History*. Oxford: Blackwell.

Keasy, K., Thompson, S. and Wright, M. 1997. 'Introduction: the corporate governance problem – competing diagnoses and solutions', in Keasy, K., Thomper, S.

and Wright, M. (eds), *Corporate Governance – Economic, Managerial, and Financial Issues*. New York: Oxford University Press.

Keenoy, T. 1990. 'HRM: a case of the wolf in sheep's clothing', *Personnel Review*, 19, 2: 363–84.

Kelly, D. and Amburgey, T. 1991. 'Organizational inertia and momentum: a dynamic model of strategic change', *Academy of Management Journal*, 34: 591–612.

Keyes, B. 1997. 'Review: ethical decision making in marketing', *Journal of the Academy of Marketing Science*, 25, 4: 362–4.

Kirichenko, O. and Koudyukin, P. 1993. 'Social partnerships in Russia: the first steps', *Economic and Industrial Democracy*, 14: 43–55.

Kitson, A. and Campbell, R. 1996. *The Ethical Organization*. London: Macmillan.

Koehn, D. 2001. 'Ethical issues connected with multi-level marketing schemes', *Journal of Business Ethics*, 29, 1/2: 153–60.

Kuhlmann, R. 2000. 'Coordination of collective bargaining policy in the European metalworking sector: a response to the challenges posed by the Euro', in Hoffman, R., Jacobi, O., Keller, B. and Weiss, M. (eds), *Transnational Industrial Relations in Europe*. Dusseldorf: Hans-Bockler-Stiftung.

Kulkarni, S. 2000. 'Environmental ethics and information asymmetry among organizational stakeholders', *Journal of Business Economics*, 27, 3: 215–28.

Laban, R. and Wolf, H. 1993. 'Large scale privatization in transition economies', *American Economic Review*, 83: 1199–210.

Laczniak, P. and Laczniak, G. 1985. *Marketing Ethics: Guidelines for Managers*. Lexington: Lexington Books.

Lampe, M. 2001. 'Mediation as an ethical adjunct of stakeholder theory', *Journal of Business Ethics*, 31, 2: 165–73.

Lamsa, A-M. 1999. 'Organizational downsizing – an ethical versus managerial viewpoint', *Leadership and Organizational Development Journal*, 20, 7: 345–53.

Larson, C.M. and Clute, R.C. (1979). 'The failure syndrome,' *American Journal of Small Business*, 4: 35–43.

Lash, S. and Friedman, J. 1992. 'Subjectivity and modernity's other', in Lash, S. and Friedman, J. (eds), *Modernity and Identity*. Oxford: Blackwell.

Lawrence, A P. 1998. *Research on Accounting Ethics, Volume 4, Pricewaterhouse Coopers*. London: JAI.

LeClair, D. 1998. 'Review: a pragmatic approach to business ethics', *Journal of the Academy of Marketing Science*, 25, 4: 364–5.

Lee, H. and Billington, C. 1995. Evolution of supply chain management models and practice at Hewlett-Packard Company, *Interfaces*, 25, 5: 42–63.

Legge, K. 1996. 'Morality bound', *People Management*, 2, 25: 34–7.

Legge, K. 1998. 'Is HRM ethical? Can HRM be ethical?', in Parker, M. (ed.), *Ethics and Organizations*. London: Sage.

Legge, K. 2000. 'The ethical context of HRM: the ethical organisation in the boundaryless world', in Winstanley, D. and Woodall, J. (eds), *Ethical Issues in Contemporary Human Resource Management*. London: Macmillan.

Leipziger, D. 2000. 'Corporate social responsibility: a focus on Latin America', in McIntosh, M. (ed.) *Visions of Ethical Business*. London: Financial Times/Prentice Hall.

Lewis, D.E. 1994. 'Major retailers warned: Reich says stores selling sweatshop goods face charges', *Boston Globe*, September 10, p. 11.

Maciver, R. and Page, C. 1961. *Society*. London: Macmillan.

Macoby, M. 2000. 'Narcissistic leaders: the incredible pros, the inevitable cons', *Harvard Business Review*, January–February: 68–78.

Manese, W.R. 1996. *Fair and Effective Employment Testing*. London: Quorum Books.

Maree, J. 1995. 'The changing role and perception of members as unions grow: the Congress of South African Trade Unions'. Paper presented at the *2nd International Conference on Emerging Union Structures*. The Swedish Institute for Work Life Research, Stockholm, 11–14 June.

Marshall, M. 1996. 'The changing face of Swedish corporatism', *Journal of Economic Issues*, 30, 3: 843–82.

Martin, L.D. 1978. 'Is an employee bill of rights needed?', in Johnson, B.M. (ed.), *The Attack on Corporate America*. Miami: University of Miami Press.

Maxwell, J., Lyon, T. and Hackett, S. 2000. 'Self-regulation and social welfare: the political economy of corporate environmentalism', *Journal of Law and Economics*, 43, 2: 583–617.

Mayer, D. and Cava, A. 1993. 'Ethics and the gender dilemma for US multi-nationals', *Journal of Business Ethics*, 12, 9: 701–8.

Maynard, M. 2001. 'Policing transnational commerce', *Journal of Business Ethics*, 30, 1: 17–27.

McDonald, K.R. 1993. 'Why privatization is not enough', *Harvard Business Review*, 71, 3: 49–59.

McIntosh, M. 2000. 'Introduction', McIntosh, M. (ed.), *Visions of Ethical Business*. London: Financial Times/Prentice Hall.

Menguc, B. 1998. 'Organizational consequences, marketing ethics and sales force supervision: further empirical evidence', *Journal of Business Ethics*, 17, 4: 333–52.

Metcalf, D. 1995. 'Workplace governance and performance', *Employee Relations*, 17, 6: 5–20.

Metcalf, D. 1999. 'The Low Pay Commission and the national minimum wage', *The Economic Journal*, 109, 453: F46–F66.

Meyer, H. 2000. 'The greening of corporate America', *Journal of Business Strategy*, 21, 1: 38–43.

Mill, J.S. 1964. *Utilitarianism; Liberty; and Representative Government*. London: Everyman.

Miller, D. 1990. *The Icarus Paradox: How Exceptional Companies Bring About Their Own Downfall: New Lessons in the Dynamics of Corporate Success, Decline, and Renewal*. New York: Harper Business.

Mintz, S.M. 1997. *Cases in Accounting Ethics and Professionalism*. New York: McGraw-Hill.

Monczka, R.M. and Trent, R.J. 1991. 'Global sourcing: a development approach', *International Journal of Purchasing and Materials Management*, 27, 2: 2–8.

Moody, K. 1997. *Workers in a Lean World*. London: Verso.

Morrissey, O. and Filatotchev, I. 2000. 'Globalisation and trade: the implications for exports from marginalised economies', *Journal of Development Studies*, 37, 2: 1–27.

Mueller, F. 1997. 'Organized industrial relations in Europe: what future?', *Organization Studies*, 18, 2: 344–8.

Munk, N. 1995. 'Now you see it, now you don't', *Forbes*, 155, 12: 42.

Munter, P. and McCaslin, T.E. 1998. 'An empirical investigation into factors affecting professional conflict in public accounting'. *Proceedings of the American Accounting Association*, 15 August, Orlando, FL.

Naser, K. 1993. *Creative Financial Accounting: Its Nature and Use.* London: Prentice Hall.

Nozick, R. 1984. 'Moral constraints and distributive justice', in Sandel, M. (ed.), *Liberalism and its Critics.* Oxford: Blackwell.

Nyaw, M-K. and Ng, I. 1994. 'A comparative analysis of ethical beliefs: a four-country study', *Journal of Business Ethics*, 13, 7: 1–13.

Oakeshott, M. 1983. *On History and Other Essays.* Oxford: Blackwell.

Oberman, W. 2000. 'The conspicuous corporation: business, public policy, and representative democracy', *Business and Society*, 39, 2: 239–44.

OECD. 1999. *OECD Principles of Corporate Governance.* Paris: OECD.

Olson, M. 1982. *The Rise and Decline of Nations: Economic Growth, Stagflation and Social Rigidities.* New Haven: Yale University Press.

Oyewole, P. 2001. 'Social costs of environmental justice associated with green marketing', *Journal of Business Ethics*, 29, 3: 239–51.

Paterson, R. 1995. 'New creative accounting', *Accountancy*, 116, 1227: 88.

Payne, D, Raiborn, C. and Askvik, J. 1997. 'A global code of business ethics', *Journal of Business Ethics*, 16: 1727–35.

Payne, S. and Wayland, R. 1999. 'Ethical obligations and diverse values assumptions in HRM', *International Journal of Manpower*, 20, 5: 297–308.

Pijper, 1994. *Creative Accounting: The Effectiveness of Financial Reporting in the UK.* London: Macmillan.

Prechel, H. 1999. 'Fighting for partnership', *Work and Occupations,* 26, 4: 539–40.

Prothero, A. and Fitchett, J. 2000. 'Greening capitalism and opportunities for a green community', *Journal of Macro Marketing*, 20, 1: 46–55.

Purcell, J. 1996. 'Contingent workers and human resource strategy: rediscovering the core periphery/dimension', *Journal of Professional Human Resource Management*, 5: 16–23.

Purcell, J. 1997. 'Pulling up the drawbridge: high commitment management and the exclusive corporation', paper presented at the Cornell Conference, *Research and Theory in SHRM: an agenda for the 21st Century*, Cornell University, Ithaca.

Rallappalli, K. 1999. 'A paradigm for the development and promulgation of a global code of marketing ethics', *Journal of Business Ethics*, 18, 1: 125–37.

Ranf, L.A. and O'Neill, M.H. 2001. 'Board composition and high-flying founders: hints of trouble to come?', *The Academy of Management Executive*, 15: 126–38.

Rao, A. and Sita, C. 1993. 'Multinational corporate social responsibility', *Journal of Business Ethics*, 12, 7: 553.

Rezaee, Z. 2000. 'Help keep the world green', *Journal of Accountancy*, 1905, 5: 57–67.

Roberts, T. and Sheail, J. 1993. 'Case study: air quality', in Berry, R.J. (ed.), *Environmental Dilemmas: Ethics and Decisions.* London: Chapman and Hall.

Rubin, H. 1993. 'Understanding the ethos of community-based development', *Public Administration Review*, 53, 5: 428–48.

Rudelius, W. and Buchholz, R.A. 1979. 'Ethical problems of purchasing managers', *Harvard Business Review*, 57: 11–14.

Saville, P. and Holdsworth, R. 1993. *Equal Opportunity Guidelines for Best Practice in Occupational Testing.* Esher, Surrey: Saville and Holdsworth.

Schlegelmilch, B. 1998. *Marketing Ethics: An Introduction.* London: International Thompson.

Schwoerer, C.E., May, D.R. and Rosen, B. 1995. 'Organizational characteristics and HRM policies on rights: exploring the patterns of connections', *Journal of Business Ethics*, 14, 7: 531–47.

Shah, A.K. 1996. 'Creative compliance in financial reporting, accounting', *Organizations and Society*, 21, 1: 23–40.

Shaub, M.K. 1988. 'Restructuring the code of professional ethics: a review of Anderson Committee Report and its implications', *Accounting Horizons*, 2, 4: 89–97.

Shlegelmilch, B. 1991. *Green, Ethical and Charitable*. Swansea: University College of Swansea.

SHRM. 1998. 'New survey looks at why people sometimes bend the rules at work', SHRM/Ethics Resource Center Business Ethics Survey (www.shrm.org).

SHRM. 2001. 'Business paying more attention to ethics: management support essential' (www.shrm.org).

SHRM/ERC Ethics Survey Snapshot. 2000. (www.shrm.org).

Singer, P. 1995. *Practical Ethics*. Cambridge: Cambridge University Press.

Singhapakdi, A., Marta, J., Rallapahi, K. and Rao, C. 2000. 'Towards an understanding of religiousness and business ethics', *Journal of Business Ethics*, 27, 4: 305–20.

Singhapakdi, A., Vitell, S., Rao, C. and Kurtz, D. 1999. 'Ethics gap', *Journal of Business Ethics*, 21, 4: 317–28.

Sisson, K. 1999. 'The "new" European social model: the end of the search for orthodoxy or another false dawn', *Employee Relations*, 21, 5: 1–54 (web copy).

Sklair, L. 1995. *Sociology of the Global System*. Hemel Hempstead: Harvester Wheatsheaf.

Sklair, L. 1996. 'Global change: regional response (book review)', *Journal of Development Studies*, 33, 1: 137–8.

Slack, N., Chambers, S., Harland, C., Harrison, A. and Johnston, R. 1995. *Operations Management*. London: Pitman Publishing.

Smith, N. 2001. 'Ethical guidelines for marketing practice', *Journal of Business Ethics*, 32, 1: 3–18.

Smith, T. 1992. *Accounting for Growth*. London: Prentice Hall.

Society of Financial Service Professionals. 2000. 'Ethical issues in the employer–employee relationship.

Solomon, R. 1992. *Ethics and Excellence: Co-operation and Integrity in Business*. Oxford: Oxford University Press.

Spence, L. 2000. 'What ethics in the employment interview?', in Winstanley, D., and Woodall, J. (eds), *Ethical Issues in Contemporary Human Resource Management*. London: Macmillan.

Stanworth, C. 2000. 'Flexible working patterns', in Winstanley, D. and Woodall, J. (eds), *Ethical Issues in Contemporary Human Resource Management*. London: Macmillan.

Starbuck, W.H. and Hedberg, B.L.T. 1977. 'Saving an organization from a stagnating environment', in Thorelli, H. (ed.), *Strategy + Structure = 3D Performance: The Strategic Planning Imperative*. Indiana: Indiana University Press.

Starbuck, W.H., Greve, A. and Hedberg, B.L.T. 1978. 'Responding to crisis', *Journal of Business Administration*, 9: 111–73.

Staw, B.M. 1981. 'The escalation of commitment to a course of action', *Academy of Management Review*, 6: 577–87.

Staw, B.M., Sandelands, L. and Dutton, J.E. 1981. 'Threat-rigidity cycles in organizational behavior: a multi-level analysis', *Administrative Sciences Quarterly*, 26: 501–24.

Stead, J. and Stead, E. 2000. 'Eco-enterprise strategy: standing for sustainability', *Journal of Business Ethics*, 24, 4: 313–29.

Strategic Finance Editors. 1999. 'Standards of ethical conduct for practitioners of management accounting and financial management', *Strategic Finance*, 81, 2: 24–90.

Strong, K., Ringer, R. and Taylor, S. 2001. The rule of stakeholder satisfaction (timeliness, honesty, empathy)', *Journal of Business Ethics*, 32, 3: 219–30.

Szaban, L. and Henderson, J. 1998. 'Globalization, institutional hegemony and industrial transformation', *Economy and Society*, 27, 4: 5575–613.

The Ethics Resource Center/Society for Human Resource Management. New York (www.shrm.org).

Tsui, A.S. 1987. 'Defining the activities and effectiveness of the human resource department: a multiple constituency approach', *Human Resource Management*, 11: 601–18.

Turner, G.B., Taylor, G.S. and Hartley, M.F. 1994. 'Ethics policies and gratuity acceptance by purchasers', *International Journal of Purchasing and Material Management*, 30, 3.

Turner, G.B., Taylor, G.S. and Hartley, M.F. 1995. 'Ethics, gratuities, and professionalization of the purchasing function', *Journal of Business Ethics*, 14, 9: 751–60.

US Congress. 1977. Senate, Subcommittee on Reports, Accounting and Management of the Committee on Government Affairs, US Government Printing Office, Washington DC.

Vartianen, J. 1998. 'Understanding Swedish social democracy: victims of success?', *Oxford Review of Economic Policy*, 14, 1: 19–39.

Verschoor, C.C. 2001. 'Strengthening the ethics of finance', *Strategic Finance*, March, 82, 9: 20–1.

Vinten, G. 2000. 'Corporate governance: the need to know', *Industrial and Commercial Training*, 32, 5: 173–8.

Visser, J. 1998. 'Two cheers for corporatism, one for the market: industrial relations, wage moderation and job growth in the Netherlands', *British Journal of Industrial Relations*, 36, 2: 269–92.

Waddock, S. 1988. 'Building successful social partnerships', *Sloane Management Review*, 29, 4: 17–24.

Waddock, S. and Post, J. 1991. 'Social entrepreneurs and catalytic change', *Public Administration Review*, 51, 5: 393–413.

Walton, S.V., Handfield, R.B. and Melnyk, S.A. 1998. 'The green supply chain: integrating suppliers into environmental management processes', *International Journal of Purchasing and Materials Management*, 34, 2: 2–11.

Warren, S.D. and Brandeis, D. 1980. 'The right to privacy', *Harvard Law Review*, December: 193–220.

Warth, R.J. 2000. 'Ethics in the accounting profession: a study', *The CPA Journal*, 70, 10: 69–70.

Watrick, S.L. and Cochran, P.L. 1985. 'The evolution of the corporate social performance model', *Academy of Management Review*, 10: 758–69.

Weiss, J.W. 1994. *Business Ethics: A Managerial, Stakeholder Approach*. Belmont: Wadsworth.

Welford, R. 1995. *Environmental Strategy and Sustainable Development*. London: Routledge.

Werhane, P.A. 1985. *Persons, Rights, and Corporations*. Englewood Cliffs: Prentice Hall.

Werhane, P.A. and Freeman, R.E. 1999. 'Business ethics: the state of the art', *International Journal of Management Review*, March: 1–16.

Weschler, L. 1999. 'Managing green', *Public Productivity and Management Review*, 23, 1: 105–8.

Whetstone, T. 2001. 'How virtue fits within business ethics', *Journal of Business Ethics*, 33, 2: 101–14.

Whitley, R. 1999. *Divergent Capitalisms: The Social Structuring and Change of Business Systems*. Oxford: Oxford University Press.

Whittington, G., Grout, P. and Jewitt, I. 1995. 'Is total auditor independence a good thing?', 1218: 75.

Wiley, C. 2000. 'Ethical standards for human resource management professionals: a comparative analysis of five major codes', *Journal of Business Ethics*, 25: 93–114.

Wilks, N. 2000. 'Be seen to be green', *Professional Engineering*, 13, 15: 40–6.

Winstanley, D. and Woodall, J. 2000a. 'The ethical dimension of human resource management', *Human Resource Management Journal*, 10, 2: 5–20.

Winstanley, D. and Woodall, J. (eds). 2000b. *Ethical Issues in Contemporary Human Resource Management*. London: Macmillan.

Winstanley, D., Woodall, J. and Heery, E. 1996. 'Business ethics and human resource management – themes and issues', *Personnel Review*, 25, 6: 5–12.

Wood, G. and Harcourt, M. 2001. 'The consequences of neo-corporatism', *International Journal of Sociology and Social Policy*, 20, 8:1–22.

Wood, S. 1996. 'High commitment management and payment systems', *Journal of Management Studies*, 33, 1: 53–78.

Wyburd, G. 1993. 'Case study: industry', in Berry, R.J. (ed.), *Environmental Dilemmas: Ethics and Decisions*. London: Chapman and Hall.

Zagaris, B. and Ohri, S. 1999. 'The emergence of an international enforcement regime in transnational competition in the Americas', *Law and Policy in International Business*, 33: 53–93.

Zajac, E.J. and Bazerman, M. 1991. 'Blind spots in industry and competitor analysis: implications of interfirm (mis)perceptions for strategic decisions', *Academy of Management Review*, 16: 37–56.

INDEX